RE-MINDED

HOW TO RENEW YOUR MIND, QUIET YOUR
SOUL, AND TRANSFORM YOUR LIFE

MARK BAKER

HOPE INK

Re-Minded: How To Renew Your Mind, Quiet Your Soul, and Transform Your Life

Copyright © 2024 by Mark Baker

All rights reserved.

No part of this publication may be reproduced, stored in a retrieval system, or transmitted in any form by any means, electronic, mechanical, photocopy, recording, scanning, or otherwise, without the prior permission of the publisher, except as provided by USA copyright law.

ISBN 9798336146813

Unless otherwise indicated, Scripture taken from the New King James Version® Copyright © 1982 by Thomas Nelson. Used by permission. All rights reserved. All italics or special emphasis on Scripture is added by the author, and does not appear in the original manuscripts, unless otherwise noted.

Hope Ink: PO Box 26811, Fresno, CA, 93729

Equipping Resources: **HopeForLifeOnline.com**

*For all those seeking
the pure truth and lasting hope
only He can give.*

*"Yet this I call to mind
and therefore I have hope."*
- Lamentations 3:21

CONTENTS

1. Therefore I Have Hope — 1
2. Re-Minded — 5
   Hopeless To Hopeful
3. Heart > Behavior — 11
   Heart Change Over Behavioral Change
4. The Hard Work of Heart Work — 21
5. Processing Pain & Trauma — 31
6. Harmful Focus — 45
   What Not To Focus On
7. Right Focus — 55
   Be Re-Minded
8. Distracted Focus — 65
   Drawn Away From The Main Things
9. Idols — 87
   Understand & Overcome Them
10. Our Fruit — 97
    A Window To Our Soul
11. Caution About Counterfeits — 117
12. A Surpassing Truth — 137
    Reaping What We Sow
13. Night & Day — 145
    Practical Changes
14. What Is "THIS" For You? — 159
15. Proactive & Reactive — 175
    Helpful Re-minders
16. Final Focus — 189

Hope For Life | Resources — 193
About the Author — 195
Notes — 197

1

THEREFORE I HAVE HOPE

Yet this I call to mind and therefore I have hope ...

— LAMENTATIONS 3:21, NIV

I once heard a Christian counselor make this statement: "Ninety percent of counseling would not need to take place if everyone lived by this one verse: *He died for all, that those who live should no longer live for themselves but for him who died for them and was raised again*" (2 Cor 5:15). While I might differ with the percentage, I love where he was going with this. There are numerous compelling and encouraging truths that can be drawn from this one verse.

> *Always remember, rejoice in, and be inspired by what God has done for you. That alone will transform your life. Remember His purposes for you, and how He designed your life to be lived—and how your faithfulness to His design plays a huge part in the fruit in your life. Living less focused on yourself—while also passionately living for God and others—will greatly help you avoid many common struggles in life, much of which are*

presented in counseling. Even better, this will also produce incredible blessings in you as well.

In addition to directing us to the wonderful principles in this passage, he presented a fascinating idea, which is isolating one verse, and how the truths therein can profoundly impact and improve our lives. He also connected this to the more specific and pivotal area of *counseling*—in which we seek to understand our personal problems, and to grow and overcome these as we learn, know, and apply the solutions.

To piggy back on his idea, I would say that a great deal of our troubles and unwanted fruit in our life would be lessened or removed—*and* replaced with incredible fruit—if everyone somehow fully lived by the principles in this one verse: *Yet this I call to mind and therefore I have hope* (Lam 3:21).

In other words, this means that if the biblical principles in this verse were truly lived out by everyone, then the need for counseling would be greatly reduced. It also means that the biblical realities in this one verse—which are expounded on throughout this book—should be emphasized and taught in all churches and in all counseling contexts. In so doing, we will be *re-minded*—which will renew our minds, still and calm our souls, and produce many desired outcomes, including overcoming countless troubles in our lives.

I realize by using this one verse that this might be seen as kind of cheating. How so? This is like being given one wish, and then wishing for an infinite amount of wishes. To put it another way: by choosing this singular Scripture, we are not limiting ourselves to just this verse. Rather, by employing the truths in this verse, we can also use *all of Scripture*, and the unlimited truths and blessings therein. Best of all, we will be able to have God Himself and His Word work powerfully in our minds, hearts, and lives.

Therefore, not only will this one verse be a focal point for us, we will take advantage of it to be *re-minded* as we practice calling to mind countless other verses and essential truths for life and blessings.

What is more, this passage will not only help us preempt numerous common struggles in our personal lives, it will also help us overcome many problems that might already exist. On top of all that, we will be able to enjoy incredible fruit, including joy, comfort, freedom, peace, and hope.

Speaking of hope ...

2

RE-MINDED

HOPELESS TO HOPEFUL

I remember my affliction and my wandering,
the bitterness and the gall.
I well remember them,
and my soul is downcast within me.
Yet this I call to mind and therefore
I have hope.

— LAMENTATIONS 3:19-21 [NIV]

Imagine if you spent an hour focusing on a book which detailed some of the most evil things humans have done to each other. What would you experience after ruminating on all of that utter wickedness? At a minimum, you would be sickened, deeply grieved, greatly disheartened, and perhaps filled with dread and despair.

In stark contrast, what would you experience if you read a book for an hour which described the most amazing and loving things humans have done for one another? You would likely be, among other things, highly encouraged and filled with awe, joy, and hope—and you might even be inspired to do loving things for those around you.

Notice, however, this vital insight: no circumstances changed in the scenario above—yet your personal experience was radically altered, if not completely reversed. So the question is: what, exactly, has the power to produce such profoundly different fruit in your life? The answer lies with the one thing that did change: *your focus*.

Can something seemingly so simple improve our lives that much? Yes, absolutely. It can, and it will. While this reality may be hard to fully believe, we find evidence of this in many places. For a specific example in the Bible—which was discussed in the first section—we can look to and learn from the night-and-day experience of Jeremiah, expressed in the verses at the beginning of this chapter: Lamentations 3:19-21.

We see how this lamenting prophet did what everyone wants to do: he went from hope*less* to *full of hope*. Even more amazing, this change transpired in just *one* verse. That is astounding. So how, exactly, did he effect such a colossal change? What was his secret? Whatever it was, there is certainly a sky-high demand for this solution all over the world. And if he could sell it in today's hope-deprived society, he would make a fortune.

As it turns out, and as you might surmise, this is not really a secret. Even better, it is *free*—and anyone can learn and apply this to their life. This includes you, me, and everyone else. While the overall process is easier said than done, we see that Jeremiah's experience was radically transformed by changing one thing: *what he set his mind on*. In other words, he was *re-minded* by reminding himself of certain truths about God, hope, grace, etc.

Jeremiah's hope transformation is even more impressive when we add more context. In the first seventeen verses of Lamentations 3, the so-called "weeping prophet" reveals several *excruciating* experiences.

To truly appreciate the magnitude of all this, it is worth your time to read these. They are so stunningly painful that they rival the suffering of Job.

One main takeaway for us here is this: the more Jeremiah focused on these traumatic experiences, the more miserable and hopeless he became. Therefore, he absolutely needed to be *re-minded*, as we all do —especially in those moments when we go through something similar (e.g., anxiety; stress; depression).

Re-Minded?

> *... to be made new in the attitude of your mind*
>
> — EPHESIANS 4:23

> *And do not be conformed to this world,*
> *but be transformed by the renewing of your mind,*
> *that you may prove what is that good and acceptable*
> *and perfect will of God.*
>
> — ROMANS 12:2

What, exactly, does *re-minded* mean? Is it the same as "reminded"?

- **RE-MINDED** = *Renewing our mind* by *calling to mind* and *believing in our heart* the many biblical truths about God and His love, grace, forgiveness, etc.

While *reminded* does not exactly equal *re-minded*, they are connected. More specifically, being reminded of key truths is crucial to being *re*-minded. How so? By correcting our focus and rightly reminding ourselves of vital truths (e.g., "this I call to mind") we can renew our minds, transform our hearts, and change the fruit in our lives.

To be clear, being re-minded is *not* about coping techniques, self-affirmations, or a "positive mental attitude" (PMA). Nor are we merely reminding ourselves of some truth. Being *re-minded* is ultimately about changing our hearts, souls, and minds—all of which make up the totality of our *inner being*.

The change and growth from being *re-minded* is done by discerning what is wrong in our thinking and focus—and in our unwanted feelings (e.g., anxiety; depression; stress)—and then *calling to mind* the right things, just like Jeremiah did, while *truly believing* and *resting in* these life-giving truths of God's Word. This is not a matter of merely correcting our focus or thoughts. Rather, we are progressively changing our hearts and minds (i.e., "renewing our mind"), which then produces the much desired fruit such as peace, comfort, and hope.

So, when it comes to Jeremiah's negative experience, it is worth emphasizing again, as it is critical to understand: Jeremiah's horrific and painful experience in the past was *not the cause* of his current misery and depression. No, his present experiences—both the good and the bad—were determined largely by *what he chose to set his mind on*:

"I *remember* my affliction ..."

"I *well remember* them ..."

"Yet this *I call to mind* ..."

This is *huge*. There are so many life-changing possibilities here. In fact, it has the potential to be life-altering—and even life-saving, literally. More specifically, this means that we can all—by consistently *correcting the focus of our minds and hearts* (i.e., being *re-minded*)—find freedom from so much stress, anxiety, trauma, depression, fear, and troubling thoughts. And, adding yet another layer of blessings, we can replace these ugly things with an abundance of hope, joy, and security.

But is this too good to be true? It can certainly seem that way, at least at first. However, as you work through this book—and as you commit to learn, believe, and truly apply the biblical truths to your mind and heart—you can personally realize the freedom and blessings that come from being *re-minded*.

So, to recap, in just the first few pages we find a handful of incredible life-changing principles:

> 1. Our present experience is *not* determined by our past experience. Yet many people live their life as if it does, leading to great harm and hopelessness.
>
> 2. Everyone can be and needs to be *re-minded*, especially in times of trouble.
>
> 3. Most of the fruit in our lives is not determined by what happens to us—but by *how we choose to respond*, by *what we choose to set our minds on*, by *what we believe*, by *where we choose to put our hope*, and by *our overall relationship with God* (e.g., Hab 3:17-19; Rom 8:5ff; Col 3:1-4; Phil 4:4-13; Lam 3:19ff; Ps 37:1-11; 42:5-6; 73:15-28; Jer 17:5-8).
>
> 4. We cannot change people or the past, but we can *always* change what we set our minds on, and we can always change our hearts and renew our minds—therefore, we can always change the fruit in our lives.

While these principles are, by themselves, incredible and life-altering, this is just the beginning. We will add more and more invaluable truths as we go along. These will further empower us to change our hearts by being *re-minded*—and they will greatly enhance our lives and our relationships with others, especially with God Himself.

APPLICATION & DISCUSSION

+ What are 2 or 3 things that stand out the most to you so far?

+ How would you explain being *re-minded* to someone else?

+ What are 2 or 3 areas you need to be *re-minded* in the most?

+ Who can be helped by being *re-minded* and changing their heart? *Those who struggle with any of the following:*

- *Anxiety, fear, and panic attacks*
- *Hopelessness, depression, and suicidal thoughts*
- *Living in shame, guilt, regret, and condemnation*
- *Insecurity and loneliness*
- *Past or current trauma (including PTSD)*
- *OCD or ADD*
- *Addictions (i.e., harmful dependencies)*
- *Anger, resentment, bitterness, and unforgiveness*
- *Over-thinking and intrusive thoughts*
- *Difficulty sleeping well and/or bad dreams*
- *Paranoia and irrational thoughts*
- *The various things described as "mental health issues"*

+ Which of the above are you wanting to overcome?

+ Is there anything else not on this list that you want to address?

3

HEART > BEHAVIOR

HEART CHANGE OVER BEHAVIORAL CHANGE

Search me, O God, and know my heart;
try me, and know my anxieties;
and see if there is any wicked way in me,
*a*nd lead me in the way everlasting.

— PSALM 139:23-24

When it comes to counseling, there are a million and one different kinds. Nevertheless, they all have one goal in common: *making changes*. Which brings up a vital question that we all need to answer: *what, exactly, needs to change?*

Unfortunately, this part of counseling—which is of utmost importance, and upon which much of life depends—is where the countless counseling ideologies clash, particularly with the Word of God (although they do in many other ways as well). As a result, they consistently go against God's perfect design for life, change, growth, love, and blessings. Not only that, they do so at those critical moments when His flawless Word and perfect ways are needed the most.

> *As for God,* **His way is perfect;**
> **the word of the Lord is flawless.**
> *He is a shield for all who take refuge in Him.*
>
> — PSALM 18:30 [NIV]

With that in mind—and as you contemplate the verses below—take time to consider what our Creator and Designer is focused on, and His emphasis on what needs to change. The overall goal is to change our *hearts*. In addition, notice that the importance God places on *changing our hearts* is directly connected to *God's Word*:

> And you shall remember that the Lord your God led you all the way these forty years in the wilderness, to humble you and test you, **to know what was in your heart, whether you would keep His commandments or not.**
>
> — DEUTERONOMY 8:2

> For the Lord does not see as man sees; *for man looks at the outward appearance,* **but the Lord looks at the heart.**
>
> — 1 SAMUEL 16:7

> Let the words of my mouth and **the meditation of my heart** *be acceptable in Your sight*, O Lord, my strength and my Redeemer.
>
> — PSALM 19:14

> ***Your word I have hidden in my heart***, *that I might not sin against You.*
>
> — PSALM 119:11

And *let the peace of God rule in your hearts*, to which also you were called in one body; *and be thankful. Let the word of Christ dwell in you richly* in all wisdom, teaching and admonishing one another in psalms and hymns and spiritual songs, *singing with grace in your hearts to the Lord.*

— COLOSSIANS 3:15-16

But the ones that fell on the good ground are those who, *having heard the word with a noble and good heart*, keep it and bear fruit with patience.

— LUKE 8:15

For the word of God is living and powerful, and sharper than any two-edged sword, piercing even to the division of soul and spirit, and of joints and marrow, and is *a discerner of the thoughts and intents of the heart.*

— HEBREWS 4:12

APPLICATION & DISCUSSION

+ After ruminating on the verses above, how would you describe the necessary connection between God's Word and His goal of changing our hearts?

+ To what degree, and in what ways does the biblical way fit with or clash against the world's approach?

The world's wisdom, just like all errant ideology, will have some truth here or there. Overall, however, it is, by definition, *opposed to God, His ways, and His Word of truth*. To prove this biblically and logically, we know that God deems "the wisdom of this world" to be "foolishness" —and the world naturally sees the perfect truths of God's Word as "foolishness" (cp. 1 Cor 1:17ff; 2:12-14; Jas 3:15-17; 4:4-5; 1 Jn 4:5-6).

> *Let no one deceive himself.* If anyone among you seems to be wise in this age, let him become a fool that he may become wise. ***For the wisdom of this world is foolishness with God.*** For it is written, "He catches the wise in their own craftiness"; and again, "The Lord knows the thoughts of the wise, *that they are futile.*"
>
> — 1 CORINTHIANS 3:18-20

∼

+ Given all that, how close is the world's wisdom to being biblical, true, and pleasing to God? And what will happen if we try to mix man's wisdom with God's Word?

Always beware of the wisdom of the world, and how the world's goals are consistently opposed to God's goals, and to God Himself. As if that is not concerning enough, know that man's wisdom, while it often appears to be for us, is functionally opposed to our wellbeing. And it naturally deceives and harms those who believe in and apply it.

These deceptive notions also occur within religious contexts— including the Church—especially when we mix man's tainted ways with God's pure truth. This mixture of truth and error is often evidenced when religious people seek to make outer changes, but do not work toward changing their hearts.

This people honors Me with their lips, but their heart is far from Me. And in vain they worship Me, *teaching as doctrines the commandments of men.*

— MARK 7:6-7

Some examples of this in the Church include: legalism; being heavy on grace, but light on truth and truth-based love; emphasizing rules and behavior, but skimping on mercy and love; blending the world's wisdom with God's Word; focusing on obtaining the right feelings and behavior, while not really focusing on changing the heart.

When it comes to biblical Christianity—and biblical counseling—one supreme goal is this: *transformation of the heart.* While that always includes a renewed mind—often by being re-minded—it is directly connected to the Word of God and our relationship with God.

Keep your heart with all diligence, for out of it *spring the issues of life.*

— PROVERBS 4:23

A sound heart is life to the body, but envy is rottenness to the bones.

— PROVERBS 14:30

As in water face reflects face, so *a man's heart reveals the man.*

— PROVERBS 27:19

If you abide in Me, and My words abide in you, you will ask what you desire, and it shall be done for you. *By this My Father is glorified, that you bear much fruit; so you will be My disciples.*

— JOHN 15:7-8

The next critical question is this: *if the goal is to change our hearts—and if the "issues of life" spring from our hearts—how do we change our hearts?*

To be sure, there is no quick fix here. Nor is this change an all-or-nothing matter. Transforming our inner-being is *a lifelong process of growth for all believers*. There are many victories *and* plenty of failures. And, ideally, we learn and grow from our failures, and then experience more victories as a result.

Put another way, heart change often involves three steps forward and one step back, and four steps forward, and two steps back. This is normal, and should be expected. If you experience this, then you are in very good company. However, what makes the difference here is *how we respond* to both our successes and failures.

Biblically speaking, this growth process is often referred to in God's Word as *sanctification*. While this undertaking is both necessary and life-giving, it always clashes with the counsel of the world.

More specifically, this overall goal of changing our heart is understood in this way:

- **Sanctification** is the *lifelong process* of being increasingly *set apart* from our trouble-causing old ways (e.g., sin; living in error; faulty thinking and beliefs)—all while *conforming our inner being to God and His Word of truth*, and reaping the blessings this produces (Gal 4:19; Eph 4:22-32; Phil 4:4-8; Col 3:1-17; Rom 8:28-29; 12:1-2; cp. Matt 15:7-9).

A specific way to understand our inner being is to realize that our heart/mind/soul contains our beliefs, desires, thoughts, and treasures (e.g., Ps 37:4; Matt 6:21; Rom 10:9-10; 12:1-2; 2 Cor 10:3-5). With this knowledge, we can specifically target these things in order to truly renew our minds and change our hearts. As we zero in on and actually change these, we will increasingly have new beliefs and desires—and, as a result, different behavior.

Better yet, if done well, these will align more and more with God, His love, and His Word—and how God brilliantly designed life to be lived. This, then, will produce different fruit: such as peace instead of anxiety, hope instead of hopelessness, security instead of insecurity, and a calmed soul instead of a troubled mind. Of course, every single human desires these things. However, true and lasting fruit here can only come from a transformed heart (e.g., Prov 4:32; Matt 6:19-21 Col 3:15-16). What is more, we need to keep in mind that, according to Jesus, the source and authority for this change process must be God and His Word, rather than man's wisdom.

> Sanctify them by Your truth. **Your word is truth.**
>
> — JOHN 17:17

However, when trying to help others overcome painful struggles like anxiety, stress, OCD, depression, anger, suffering, and trauma—instead of relying on the right understanding of the heart, and seeking to rightly change our hearts—one main thing many people heavily rely on is *coping techniques*. What are these? In general, and pertinent to our topic, they are methods that are designed to help us manage our unwanted thoughts and feelings, largely by distracting us and changing our focus.

While this can certainly be helpful in a pinch, unfortunately, any relief is *only temporary*. More importantly, *the actual cause* of our distress is left unaddressed, which often leads to ongoing harm. How so? Because of this universally understood reality:

- *If we do not address and resolve the **cause** of a problem, the problem will remain, and will likely get worse and worse*

This is worth saying again, albeit in a slight different way: if we do not deal with and overcome these issues *in our heart*, the problems will not only stay the same, *they will usually get worse* (cp. Matt 15:8-9; Lk 6:45; Prov 4:23).

To illustrate this, several years ago a Christian therapist came to me for help regarding her anxiety, and to learn how to help others as well. During this process I asked her how she counsels people who struggle with this, and similar problems. She somewhat sheepishly replied that all she offered were coping techniques.

However, to her credit, this caring young lady was very concerned about the fleeting benefits of her methodology, and how it never really addressed the heart of the individual, nor the cause of the problems. Better yet, she was very eager to implement what she was now applying to her own heart. And, as a result of her new sanctification and equipping, she changed her approach in how she counseled others, at least in this area.

This is a great example of the supreme importance of *rightly changing our inner being*, and not merely our feelings or outer behavior, including our focus. Coping mechanisms may help us cope, but *only for a moment*. The far bigger concern is that they do not address what is *causing* our pain and stress. Therefore, they do not solve the actual problems.

To further illustrate this, I have had more than one individual contact me for counseling and plead with me at the very beginning: "Whatever you do, please do not give me coping techniques!" Why are they so adamant about this? Because that is mainly what they have received from previous counseling—and, after using these techniques for a little while, they stopped working, if they ever worked at all. This only resulted in their being even more hopeless and distressed.

However, they are greatly relieved to see how God's Word addresses the cause of our problems, while also providing the solutions. They are also motivated, perhaps more than most, to learn and apply these biblical principles to their lives.

To be clear, we are not against certain methods of coping (at least their temporary use). But we are against the harmful ones (more on this later)—and the over-reliance on them—as well as the use of these without addressing and overcoming the actual cause of the problems.

So, while *focus* is a central topic, we do not want focus to be merely a technique we practice when we are stressed, anxious, or depressed—although changing our focus is critical in those moments (e.g., being *re-minded*).

We must always keep in mind that the overall goal—which is also God's goal for us—is *to change our heart, mind, and soul*, particularly by *becoming more like Christ*. This book is dedicated to this very purpose, which is also God's purpose for all of us (1 Sam 16:7; Ps 19:14; Prov 2:1ff; 4:23; Lk 6:45; Matt 6:19-21; Col 3:1-4; Jas 4:1-3).

> *My little children, for whom I labor in birth again until Christ is formed in you ...*
>
> — GALATIANS 4:19

4

THE HARD WORK OF HEART WORK

Keep your heart **with all diligence**...

— PROVERBS 4:23

While God's goal for us is to renew our minds and change our hearts, we are to also "keep (our) heart with all diligence." How is this done? There are many things that go into it, as discussed in previous chapters, but it primarily includes increasingly *believing the truth*—especially the truth about God—*and* yielding to and trusting the God of truth.

> But we ought always to thank God for you, brothers loved by the Lord, because from the beginning God chose you to be saved *through the sanctifying work of the Spirit* and **through belief in the truth**.
>
> — 2 THESSALONIANS 2:13 [NIV]

Charles Spurgeon, in the following quote, helps us connect the dots between changing our inner being and how this will change the fruit in our lives.

> To enjoy peace, our unbelieving thoughts must be stilled, and we must learn that the Lord reigns.[1]
>
> — C.H. SPURGEON

To put it another way, we can we "enjoy peace" by:

- *Stilling our "unbelieving thoughts."*

- *Harmonizing the beliefs of our hearts with the reality of God's character.*

- *Harmonizing our shortsighted goals with the supremacy of God's goals* (cp. Is 55:6-9; Matt 16:23; 2 Cor 1:8-9; 4:16-18; 12:7-10; Eph 4:22-5:2; Heb 12:1-15)."Harmonizing" here means: *conforming our goals, desires, and beliefs so that they are in agreement with God's goals, desires, and character.*

While easier said than done, this is the path we all must take. And this is never more true than when we are troubled inwardly (cp. Ps 37:1-11; 42; 73:14-28; Lam 3:19-26).

∼

APPLICATION & DISCUSSION

+ What would a person's life and fruit look like if, in theory, they perfectly harmonized their goals, desires, and beliefs with God's goals, desires, and character?

+ What does that tell us about the power of this one thing in our life?

+ What are your most common "unbelieving thoughts" you would love to overcome?

+ In what ways do you intentionally work to calm or still these thoughts? And how much time do you invest in this?

+ Which verses, if any, help you the most?

A Psalm Short & Sweet

Similar to Spurgeon's quote, in the 131st Psalm, God reveals some ways we can each change our heart, mind, *and* fruit—*especially in times of distress*. We can glean from the overall Psalm that King David likely went through a significant struggle before writing this—and that he wrestled in his heart with the truth, particularly the truth about God Himself.

The good news here is that David eventually prevailed. How so? He was able to do what everyone wants: *to calm and quiet his soul, and, therefore, to enjoy great peace of mind.*

> *Lord, my heart is not haughty, nor my eyes lofty.*
> *Neither do I concern myself with great matters,*
> *nor with things too profound for me.*
> **Surely I have calmed and quieted my soul,**
> *like a weaned child with his mother;*
> *like a weaned child is my soul within me.*
> *O Israel,* **hope in the Lord**
> *from this time forth and* forever.
>
> — PSALM 131:1-3

The first verse seems to indicate that David was greatly humbled, and that he likely learned a very painful and powerful lesson: *do not take on matters that are too "great" for you.*

This reality is so critical for all of us to understand. Why? Because our stress, hopelessness, and anxiety often come when we take on *too much* in our life, or even what is impossible. Some examples of this are laid out in the following (not exhaustive) list.

Contributing Factors For Anxiety & Hopelessness

- Trying to earn love — from God, or from others
- Trying to change people
- Trying to change the past
- Trying to fix things we cannot fix
- Trying to go through life without grieving and processing our distress with God
- Focusing on and fretting over circumstances we cannot change
- Not asking for help (when it is wise and necessary to do so)
- Not delegating responsibilities (when it would be wise and helpful to do so)
- Trying to control things we do not control
- Trying to control everything
- Trying to find our value, lasting peace, and security through our performance
- Taking on too much responsibility — more specifically, taking on things that are not our responsibility (i.e., God's responsibility, or that of other people)
- Trying to be perfect
- Trying to fully comprehend things we will likely never grasp (cp. Deut 29:29)

APPLICATION & DISCUSSION

+ Which of the things on this list do you tend to struggle with?

+ How would you explain to another person how these lead to stress, anxiety, and insecurity?

+ In what ways might these things be connected to *pride* in a person's life—a struggle to yield to and trust God (e.g., being controlling)?

+ In what specific ways could a person be *re-minded* here, which would lead them out of this turmoil and to a calm and quieted soul?

+ How would you explain how these also lead to *depression*? [Hint: Depression is the ugly feeling we experience when we see something as *hopeless* in our life.]

If we take on something that is *impossible*—like trying to be perfect, earn love, change other people, or control things we cannot control—then, for obvious reasons, this will lead to *hopelessness*. In other words, we will experience *depression* (i.e., hopelessness) to the degree we invest our time, focus, and energy in that which is *impossible*.

Conversely, there are times when it can be very good to take on things that stretch us—like learning a new skill, making new friends, or being challenged by a difficult job or project. Such things often test us, humble us, teach us, refine us, and cause us to grow as we increasingly depend on God (cp. Deut 8:1-5). Yet, that is different from taking on that which we cannot do, are not called to do, or is simply impossible.

In the second verse of Psalm 131, we see that David—while likely in the midst of profound inner turmoil—went through *a necessary and vital process* of *calming and quieting his soul*, which is similar to *stilling unbelieving thoughts*. And, just like the process of weaning a child, effecting a longterm peace in his heart did not happen in a moment.

It cannot be emphasized enough, at least for some of us, that this desired change involves a *process*. Why? Because our tendency is to look for a quick fix, to be impatient, to quit when it does not happen soon enough, and to place unreasonable expectations on ourselves and the outcome. Or, we develop a pattern where we focus on just getting rid of our unwanted thoughts and feelings, rather than on addressing *the cause* of these undesirable things.

+ Which of these might apply to you?

The reality is that success here takes time and patience—through the hard work of transforming our hearts—which always includes *renewing our minds.*

> *Do not conform to the pattern of this world,*
> *but be transformed by the renewing of your mind ...*
>
> — ROMANS 12:2

What David says in the second verse is more important than the first: "Surely *I* have calmed and quieted my soul." Did this mean he did not need God, or that he did it on his own? Of course not. What it tells us is that there are things *we can do*—and *need to do*—in order to calm and quiet our souls. That alone, the fact that there are things we *can* do, should give us so much hope.

Put another way, we do not have to wait for our circumstances to change, so that *only then* can we have peace. Nor do we have to wait around for God to supernaturally zap us with stillness of mind (it does *not* say, "Surely *God* has calmed and quieted my soul").

Rather, God gives us profoundly good news: there are many things we can do, should do, and *get* to do in the midst of troubling times. Not only that, these things lead to great relief of our distress—and to peace, comfort, and joy—as well as to many other blessings (e.g., Lam 3:21; Is 26:3; Phil 4:4-8).

To be abundantly clear, *we always need God*. He is always needed here, and everywhere else. And, of course, we can do nothing apart from Him (Jn 15:1ff). However, as we are *re-minded*—as we turn to God, and as we seek Him and increasingly harmonize our beliefs with the truth about God—we can know more and more peace, hope, and joy in our heart.

So, in all this, just like a weaned child, King David was eventually able to reconcile at least two conflicting things in his heart:

- What he wanted with what God wanted
- What he thought was best with what God *knows* is best

This, then, resulted in a quieted mind, a satisfied soul, and a heart at peace. Best of all, at least for you and me, this is possible for every one of us as well.

It is worth noting that this harmony was not achieved by negotiating some middle ground with God—or because God gave in to David's demands—or because his circumstances finally improved. Nor was peace realized because David finally figured everything out, or because he received true justice. And it certainly did not come through some kind of mystical meditation (e.g., contemplative prayer; entering into the "Presence" of God).

No, David's troubled soul was "calmed and quieted" as he *humbled himself*, and as he increasingly *trusted God*—especially by trusting Him with the things he did not understand (Prov 3:5-6)—and because he ultimately *yielded to God and to His will*. This life-changing lesson is more than worth the wait.

> The deepest spiritual lessons are not learned by his letting us have our way in the end, but by his making us wait, bearing with us in love and patience until we are able to honestly pray what he taught his disciples to pray: *Thy will be done.*[2]
>
> — ELISABETH ELLIOT

All of this is not, of course, limited to this one instance with David. We find these same amazing principles elsewhere in Scripture. In the following verses we see the connection between distress, and then turning to and trusting God, and the resulting peace.

> When my soul fainted within me, **I remembered the Lord; and my prayer went up to You**, into Your holy temple.
>
> — JONAH 2:7

> You will keep him in **perfect peace**, whose mind is stayed on You, **because he trusts in You.**
>
> — ISAIAH 26:3

> Then they cried out to the Lord in their trouble, and **He delivered them out of their distresses**.
>
> — PSALM 107:6

> Let not your heart be troubled; **you believe in God, believe also in Me.**
>
> — JOHN 14:1

> *Now* may the God of hope fill you with all joy and peace *in believing*, that you may abound in hope by the power of the Holy Spirit.
>
> — ROMANS 15:13

Therefore, in *our* personal times of turmoil, it is frequently necessary that *we* go through a similar heart-changing process, that of wrestling with the truth, and with God Himself. Yet, at the same time, this is also the road less traveled when it comes to overcoming common struggles like anxiety, stress, pain, and relationship issues.

Again, this process of reconciling things in our hearts is not new, nor is it foreign to Scripture. Many struggling individuals did this throughout God's Word. For example, not only did the prophet Jeremiah do something like this in the book of Lamentations (e.g., lamenting, grieving, and being re-minded), several psalmists did as well.

You, too, will certainly need to do this, perhaps many times in your life (1 Sam 1:10-16; Ps 6; 10; 13; Lk 22:44; Phil 4:6ff; Col 4:12; Heb 5:14). However, whether you choose to walk this path or not, and how well you do so, is entirely up to you—all with God's abundant love and power, of course.

5

PROCESSING PAIN & TRAUMA

O Lord, God of my salvation,
I have cried out day and night before You.
Let my prayer come before You;
Incline Your ear to my cry.
For my soul is full of troubles,
And my life draws near to the grave.

— PSALM 88:1-3

In general, the focus on dealing with trauma has spiked in the last few years. This has resulted in a mixed bag, with some good things and some not so good things, which is par for the course when it comes to new movements, and whenever people are involved.

A couple of good things here include shining light on a much neglected area of life, and the many caring individuals who want to help others. However, as is often the case, many significant weaknesses have come with this as well. In particular, there are several shortcomings when it comes to accurately understanding the actual problems, and, more importantly, in knowing and applying the right solutions.

While our desire is to sufficiently equip others for this very challenging area of life, we will also try to keep things relatively simple in our approach. Here is an easier-said-than-done *simplified summary* of how we can grieve and process angst and trauma:

- First, we need to honestly and accurately acknowledge any hurt, stress, and extreme difficulties in our life—while turning to God with our grief, distress, and sorrow.

- Next, we need to talk with God, pour out our hearts to Him, and grieve and lament with God Himself. Through this *process,* we can progressively overcome the pain, and increasingly calm and quiet our soul, while putting more and more hope in God and His superlative ways (cp. Phil 4:6-8; Is 55:8-9; Ps 10; 73:15-26; 2 Cor 4:16-18).

In addition, most suffering and trauma involves *significant sin* on someone's part, and, therefore, the *absolute need for forgiveness*—to give and receive true forgiveness. For example:

- Wherever sin is involved, we need to thoroughly and biblically forgive *anyone* who has sinned against us and caused our pain; forgiving others also involves a process (Matt 18:21-35; Mk 11:25; Eph 4:31-32).

- When it comes to *our* personal sin, we need to contritely confess, ask for, receive, and live in God's full forgiveness—and truly repent of our sin—as well as live in His grace, truth, and love; and, wherever appropriate, we need to ask for forgiveness from those we have sinned against (Ps 32; 38; 51; Prov 28:13; 2 Cor 7:10-11; Jas 4:8-9; 1 Jn 1:5-10).

However, when it comes to overcoming past pain through forgiveness, this pivotal area of life is often a stumbling block for many. There are four main causes for this, which include:

1. Erroneous understanding of forgiveness

2. Resistance or refusal to truly and fully forgive

3. People who discourage us from forgiving (there are segments of our society—and in counseling—who thrive on keeping others stuck in a victim mentality)

4. A struggle to believe and receive full forgiveness from God (we get stuck in shame, guilt, and condemnation, while often beating ourselves up)

APPLICATION & DISCUSSION

+ How much does your past pain and trauma involve the need to forgive? And how well have you truly forgiven these painful offenses?

+ Which of the four stumbling blocks above might apply to you?

+ In what ways have any of these hindered your ability to overcome and heal from past pain?

+ What, specifically, are you going to do about this?

For all of the reasons above, and more, we have written a great deal of material on forgiveness. These biblical truths benefit people in many ways. In particular, it helps them avoid the errors about forgiveness that are taught inside and outside of the Church (e.g., forgiving means we have to trust the offender; forgiveness equals reconciliation; the need to forgive ourselves). Best of all, the right understanding here frees others to truly overcome much of the pain and trauma in their lives.

Questions & Objections

All of these verses and principles about processing and overcoming pain naturally produce questions, and even some objections. Therefore, to gain a much better understanding, we will address a few of these below.

"What are some things we should avoid when we experience suffering?"

Here are five main things *not* to do with trauma/distress:

1. Stuffing — Do not stuff the pain down. (Eph 4:26-27)

2. Avoidance — Do not avoid addressing your problems and distress (cp. Ps 5-7; 42; 88; Matt 11:28-30; Gal 6:2)—yet you do need to avoid longterm "survival-mode."

3. Isolation — Do not isolate—and make sure you surround yourself with the right people (2 Tim 2:22; cp. Ps 1:1-3; 62; 73; Prov 27:6). There is, of course, time to be alone with God and His Word, and to process our pain with God Himself.

4. Faulty Dependencies — Do not develop dependencies on temporary things, or overtly harmful things (e.g., escapism; addictions; coping rather than changing your heart). Rather, directly address *the cause* of your pain and problems, and, therefore, develop the right kind of dependencies (Jer 2:13; 17:5-8; Rom 1:25; Rom 15:4, 13).

5. Faulty Sources — Do not go to bad sources of counsel and help. Especially avoid the approaches that might seem to work, but are really from the "world's wisdom," and "what is falsely called knowledge" (e.g., unbiblical meditation; humanistic psychology; New Age ideology; Ps 1:1-3; Prov 14:12; 1 Cor 3:18-20; Col 2:4, 8; 1 Tim 6:20-21). In addition, there are many who claim to have the biblical or Christian approach, but they distort and twist the truths therein (e.g., blaming everything on demons and/or sin).

APPLICATION & DISCUSSION

+ Which of these faulty ways are the most common responses for people in general?

+ Which ones are the most harmful? Why?

+ When you are going through pain and difficulties, which of the above applies the most to you?

+ How different would your life be if you had avoided all of these harmful responses?

"What are some biblical examples of grieving and processing pain?"

There are many wonderful people throughout God's Word who not only walked through *extreme* pain and grief, but they also truly processed those things with God. Therefore, spend ample time meditating on these examples. Along with greatly encouraging you, they will direct you in how to personally handle the suffering and heartache in your life.

The people went to Bethel, where *they sat before God until evening, raising their voices and weeping bitterly.*

— JUDGES 21:2 [NIV]

In bitterness of soul Hannah wept much and prayed to the Lord ... I have been praying here out of my great anguish and grief.

— 1 SAMUEL 1:10 ...16 [NIV]

As he finished speaking, the king's sons came in, *wailing loudly.* The king, too, and *all his servants wept very bitterly.*

— 2 SAMUEL 13:36 [NIV]

Hezekiah turned his face to the wall and prayed to the Lord, "Remember, O Lord, how I have walked before you faithfully and with wholehearted devotion and have done what is good in your eyes." And *Hezekiah wept bitterly.*

— 2 KINGS 20:2-3 [NIV]

My tears have been my food day and night, while men say to me all day long, "Where is your God?" These things I remember as I pour out my soul ...

— PSALM 42:3-4 [NIV]

I cry aloud to the Lord; I lift up my voice to the Lord for mercy. I pour out my complaint before Him; before Him I tell my trouble.

— PSALM 142:1-2 [NIV]

"Okay, but how, exactly, do I process these things?"

There is no exact formula for grieving and processing pain. However, when it comes to ways in which we can process our suffering, we see several *vital opportunities* for us in Scripture (revealed in the previous verses). For example:

- Turning to God our Father in the midst of our pain
- Crying out to the Lord, and pouring our hearts out to Him
- Feeling and expressing intense emotions like anguish and sorrow
- Wholeheartedly and honestly praying to the Lord
- Asking God for mercy, strength, comfort, and help
- Mourning pain and loss
- Waiting on God
- Putting our hope in what is "unseen" and eternal, rather than what is "seen" and temporary (2 Cor 4:16-18)
- Voicing our specific troubles and griefs to the Lord
- Relinquishing anything that is harmful and not of God
- Making God our refuge and our rock
- Reconciling our shortsighted ways with God's ways
- Filling our minds and hearts with God's Word of life
- Yielding and surrendering to the Lord
- Deepening our dependence on God, His love, and truth
- Rejoicing in, giving thanks to, and worshiping God
- Putting more hope in God, His Word, His ways, and His timing
- Entrusting ourselves and our concerns to God

+ Which of these have you already relied on? Which ones are the most helpful?

+ Which of these do you want to increasingly take advantage of and put into practice? Why those particular areas?

To be clear, you do not have to do *all* of these things. However, each one has enormous potential to help you process and overcome any distress and trauma in your life. Therefore, seek the ones that apply to you and your circumstances—and the last eight are especially helpful for *everyone* and *every situation*.

After processing this to some degree, we eventually get to the place where we put into practice a central theme of this book:

- Consistently turning our focus away from past pain while also calling to mind and truly believing the right things (Lam 3:21; Phil 4:8). This includes taking captive unwanted thoughts and making them obedient to Christ (2 Cor 10:3-5).

All of the above possibilities are healthy, good, and greatly beneficial. In time, by persevering and faithfully *processing our pain with God*, we can and will produce wonderful fruit, including a comforted and quieted soul.

On the other hand, if we do not walk steadily through this process, then we will likely experience stunted growth, further harm, and even more troubles in life, including in our relationships.

This increased distress is commonly referred to as PTSD. Fortunately, we have numerous things we can do in the midst of and in response to our suffering.

"Yeah, but ... I want to know why this happened!"

Yes, we would all like to know the "whys" and "hows" of our personal suffering. Some examples of common and valid questions regarding this are:

- Why did God allow this?
- How long will this last, or why is this lasting so long?
- Where was Jesus in this?
- If God is love, if He is for me, how can He allow such a painful and evil thing to happen?
- Why did that person do such a horrible thing to me?
- Where's the justice?
- How can people who call themselves Christians do such horrible things to others?

While we can certainly ask these questions and seek to understand—as many of the Psalmists did—we should not expect to receive *all* the answers we long for. Therefore, here is what we can and need to do in our suffering—which is absolutely essential for grieving, healing, and overcoming:

- We can make reasonable attempts to understand our specific suffering, but *we also need to ultimately trust God with all that we cannot grasp, or find answers to* (Deut 29:29; Prov 3:5-6; Ps 37; 73:23-26; Is 26:3 Jn 16:33).

In addition, it is very beneficial for us to gain an understanding of *general* suffering—for example: learning why God allows suffering in the lives of everyone, *and* what God is often doing through our pain (e.g., 2 Cor 1:8-9; Heb 12:5-13).

"Yeah, but ... all of that is really hard to do!"

Yes, this is certainly not easy, but it is necessary. And we absolutely need a lot of help when it comes to grieving, processing our pain, forgiving, and yielding to God. How much more when there has been a great deal of suffering? Therefore, growing in the following five powerful things will greatly aid and empower us here.

> 1. **Knowing** God—and, more specifically, *being certain of His love for us*, and of *the overall goodness of His divine character*. (Rom 5:5; 8:28-32; 2 Tim 1:12; Heb 12:5-13; 1 Pet 5:7)
>
> 2. **Trusting** God—especially when we do not fully understand our circumstances. (Prov 3:5-6; Is 26:3; Rom 15:13)
>
> 3. **Desiring** God's ways over our ways—as we gladly and confidently admit that His ways are *infinitely better* than our ways. (Is 55:8-9; Jn 15:1ff; Heb 12:5-13)
>
> 4. **Realizing** that there is so much more going on than what we see or feel right now, *especially in eternity*. (Job; Ps 73:15-28; Heb 11; 2 Cor 4:16-18)
>
> 5. **Convinced** that *God is more than "able"* to do what is right and best, not just now or as we see things, but overall, and for His purposes (e.g., "for that day," Eph 3:20-21)

> That is why I am suffering as I am. Yet I am not ashamed, because ***I know** whom **I have believed**, and **am** convinced **that** he is able* to guard what *I have* entrusted to him *for that day.*
>
> — 2 TIMOTHY 1:12 [NIV]

Growing in these things is easier said than done (another theme of this book, not to mention life as a whole), and we can all improve in these areas. In addition, we should not view it as "all or nothing," that is: either we fully trust God, or we don't trust Him at all. There is a spectrum with all five (e.g., 0 to 10).

However, these are very helpful in pinpointing the specific ways in which we can and need to grow. Better yet, to the degree we grow in each area, we will be more successful in processing and overcoming life's difficulties, yielding to God, and calming and quieting our souls.

APPLICATION & DISCUSSION

+ Of the five areas mentioned, what are the top two or three you want to grow in the most? Why those ones?

+ What are some specific things you are going to do in order to grow here?

+ What do you think has hindered your ability in any of these five areas?

+ In what ways do you tend to look for a quick fix, rather than diligently walking with God through suffering?

To be clear, this process is not a temporary surrender, nor are we yielding to a mystical, unknown God. Rather, *we get to put our hope in the God of hope*—not merely in the moment, but more and more, and for the rest of our lives, just as the last verse of Psalm 131 states.

> *O Israel, **hope in the Lord**
> From this time forth and forever.*
>
> — PSALM 131:3

> *Why are you cast down, O my soul?
> And why are you disquieted within me?
> **Hope in God**, for I shall yet praise Him
> For the help of His countenance.*
>
> — PSALM 42:5

As you can see, this process involves *heart work*, which is also *hard work*. However, while this can be arduous, it will, in due time, produce a multitude of blessings. Better yet, it will make life much, *much* easier in the long run.

This timeline and dynamic of being "trained" through difficulties brings us to what could be the most pivotal verse for understanding this very topic (i.e., suffering, and how to overcome it).

> No discipline seems pleasant *at the time*, but *painful.* **Later on, however, it produces a harvest of righteousness and peace for those who have been trained by it.**
>
> — HEBREWS 12:11 [NIV]

Are you in need of such work in your heart, particularly in relation to hardship and suffering? If so, then you are in very good company. In fact, this is common in the Christian walk, or at least it should be, especially when we are hit the hardest.

Even though it always involves pain, the overall "discipline" process can always produce blessings—at least to the degree we "have been trained by it" (Heb 12:11). On the other hand, if we do not go through this, then we will likely be stunted in our spiritual growth (cp. Heb 5:12-14; Phil 1:9-11).

Unfortunately, it is our nature to bypass this much needed heart work. Therefore, we end up avoiding this universally needed process —or we depend on shortcuts, temporary fixes, the world's wisdom, and false teachings, including mystical methods, like counterfeit forms of meditation (much more on this later). As a result, we will frequently go up and down—but increasingly down.

Thankfully, there are numerous biblical, God-designed solutions for a "disquieted" soul, a crushed spirit, a broken heart, a troubled mind, and traumatic experiences. And they all involve the unlimited blessings that are found in God Himself and His Word. We will learn many of these in the pages of this book.

Nevertheless, there is a very common mindset when it comes to the hard work of heart work, which goes something like this: "Yeah, I see that, including the verses and all. But what I want to know is, how can I get rid of my anxiety, stress, grief, and hopelessness—and replace it with peace, hope, joy—*without having to do all of that heart work?*"

Few people, if any, will come right out and say such things. And hardly any realize that this is, in fact, their mindset when it comes to change and growth. Yet this is at the top of the list, if not the number one reason why people struggle to overcome their painful experiences and troubled minds.

APPLICATION & DISCUSSION

+ In what ways, and to what degree, does this faulty mindset apply to you?

On the other hand, there are those who are very willing to work hard, but they are given *faulty instruction*—which gives them *false hope*, and leads to unnecessary frustration and failure. As a result, they are often tempted to quit, and many do.

+ In what ways might any of this be true of you, at least in the past?

+ When it comes to helping you change your heart and overcome troubles in life, what are the most important truths you will take away from this chapter?

+ How would you explain the hard work of heart work to someone who is struggling, and how this process actually gives us an abundance of hope?

6

HARMFUL FOCUS
WHAT NOT TO FOCUS ON

My soul still remembers *a*nd sinks within me.

— LAMENTATIONS 3:20

Turn away my eyes from looking at worthless things,
And revive me in Your way.

— PSALM 119:37

For to be carnally minded *is* **death** ...

— ROMANS 8:6

When I was about ten years old, I made one of the more foolhardy decisions of my life. My mom let me spend the night at a friend's house, which was great. However, a bunch of us kids decided to sneak over to another kid's house to watch a movie that was explicitly banned by everyone's parents—and warned against by much of society. But, in my defense, what self-respecting, rebellious pre-teen can resist a forbidden movie, right?

What was the movie that was so alluring to foolish pre-adolescents? It was *The Exorcist*. If you know anything about it, you know how evil, scary, and inappropriate it is for 10 year old boys, not to mention for any human being.

The net effect of watching it was that I could not sleep at all that night, as I could not get the demonic imagery out of my mind. I still remember freaking out every two minutes by seeing the shadows cast into the room I was laying in, and how they shifted as the bushes outside were blown by the wind.

I didn't just not sleep, I was terrified and petrified the entire night, with horrible thoughts continually running in my mind. Worse, I did not sleep all that well for months. And who knows how many nightmares I had. It was horrible in numerous ways.

Nevertheless, I learned a painful, yet powerful, life-changing lesson even at that age: *what you allow into your mind can greatly harm you and dominate your thinking and your life for long periods of time.* As a result, this chapter will be dedicated to foolish ten year olds, and, more specifically, to learning about what *not* to focus on, *and* how to improve in this area.

So, before we get to the good stuff to focus on, our first step in being *re-minded* will be to address the negative side of this reality. We need to understand that by occupying our minds and hearts with the following harmful things, *we will be guaranteed to produce painful fruit in our lives*, such as: anxiety; stress; depression; resentment; insecurity; and fear.

Harmful Things To Focus On

+ As you read the following list, *rate your focus for each item on a scale of 0 to 10, ten being the highest (most focus)*. To what degree do the following things occupy your mind?

____ **Complaining & Grumbling** | (Phil 2:14; Num 14:1-4)

____ **Comparing Yourself To Others** | Your place in life; appearance; performance; family; job/career; how many friends or followers you have; (cp. Ps 73:3ff)

____ **What Others Think Of You** | Or what *you think* others think of you (i.e., the fear of man; Prov 29:25; Jer 17:5-8)

____ **Regret** | (cp. 2 Cor 7:10; Phil 3:13-14)

____ **Doing Things *Your Way*** | Often includes stubbornness or pride, rather than yielding to and trusting God and *His ways* (cp. Is 55:8-9; Jer 2:13; Matt 16:23; Jas 4:1-10)

____ **Frequently Criticizing Others** | Easily finding fault in people. There is a time to observe and discern weakness and problems in others, and this can be very necessary and helpful *if* we handle it appropriately, with grace, truth, and love (Rom 15:1-6; Gal 6:1; Eph 4:15-16; Jas 5:19-20).

____ **Frequently Criticizing Yourself** | Being quick to find fault in yourself, and your performance. It's important to *objectively* observe and discern the weaknesses and sin in your life (Ps 139:23-24; 2 Cor 13:5; Rom 12:3). If you handle this well, with truth *and* grace, it will be highly beneficial.

____ **Social Media** | This can expose you to a great deal of negativity, sin, deception, comparing, mockery, hatred, demonizing everything that is godly and biblical, exalting what is evil, and perverting and subverting the eight wonderful things in Philippians 4:8 (e.g., whatever is true, noble, pure, etc.).

____ **News & Media** | We do want to be *accurately* informed, but the downfall here is relying on bad and biased sources, and focusing *too much* on the news, and on negative things, while not dwelling on the many good things.

____ **Living In Condemnation** | Shame and guilt, rather than grace and truth (cp. Rom 8:1ff; Heb 4:16; 1 Jn 1:9; Jn 1:14, 17; 2 Cor 3:5ff)

____ **Worldly Wisdom** | Seeking and believing in the counsel and wisdom of *the world* ("man's wisdom"; Ps 1:1-3; Col 2:8; 1 Cor 17ff; 3:18-20; Jas 3:15; 4:4-5; 1 Jn 4:1-6).

____ **Excessive Negativity** | The negative things in life (like perpetually glum Eeyore in Winnie the Pooh). This struggle is often combined with neglecting the positive things (cp. Lam 3:19-21; Phil 4:8; Heb 12:1ff).

____ **Lust, Envy, Jealousy** | (Prov 6:16-19)

____ **Self-Centeredness** | Thinking of yourself too much, while often lacking concern for others and their well-being, or thinking much about God and His ways (Jas 3:14-16; 2 Tim 3:1ff; cp. 2 Cor 5:15)

____ **Unrealistic Expectations** | Those others have for you (real or perceived)

____ **Criticism** | Hurtful words from others (1 Kgs 21:1ff)

____ **Living In Fear** | cp. Matt 10:31; 1 Jn 4:18; Ps 37:1ff)

____ **False needs** | For example: "I need people to like me;" "I need to be perfect;" "I need ____ in order to be content;" "I need my spouse to perform better in order to fill my love tank;" obsessing over things you think need to happen (e.g., *OCD*); "I need _____ to cope with my stress."

____ **Others' Performance** | Fretting over what *others* are doing or not doing—while not focusing on what *you* are responsible for and called to do (cp. Ps 37; 73; Col 3:23-24)

____ **Self-Pity** | (e.g., 1 Kgs 21:4; Jon 4:1-5)

____ **Sinful Desires** | What your sinful nature desires (Rom 8:5ff; Gal 5:19-21; 6:7-8)

____ **Fantasizing** | In a negative, self-focused, and sinful way

____ **Your Performance** | Especially compared to others, with unreasonable expectations of yourself—or identifying too much with your performance, with a lack of living in grace.

____ **Control** | Trying to control what you cannot control.

____ **Changing Others** | Trying to change other people.

____ **Circumstances** | *Rather than* focusing on God's sufficient grace and love for you, and on what you can do in the midst of these circumstances (e.g., 1 Jn 4:16-18; 2 Cor 3:5ff; 4:16-18; 2 Pet 1:3-4; 2 Tim 3:15-17).

____ **Resentment** | Focusing on the wrongdoing and sins of others against you, or against your loved ones — In other words, living with unforgiveness and resentment (cp. Eph 4:31-32; Col 3:12-14). [We have much more on the topic of forgiveness, including: *Forgiveness: A Biblical Handbook*]

____ **Current Sin** | Any *current sin* in your life, in an unhealthy and ungodly way (e.g., unrepentantly indulging in one or more sins; cp. Gal 6:7-8)

____ **Past Sin** | Your *past sin*, and beating yourself up over past failures (e.g., living in condemnation rather than grace *and* truth). While "forgiving yourself" is a common suggestion, it is *never* the solution. Why? Because it is not biblical, nor is it possible. However, there are very real problems that underlie this faulty notion, and there are biblical solutions to these real and painful problems.

____ **The Past** | Focusing on and regretting what went wrong, what did not happen, what you could have done or should have done differently, etc. (Is 43:18-19)

~

> Brethren, I do not count myself to have apprehended; but one thing I do, *forgetting those things which are behind* and *reaching forward* to those things which are ahead, *I press toward the goal for the prize of the upward call of God in Christ Jesus.*
>
> — PHILIPPIANS 3:13-14

If you have not done so already, go back and rate your focus for each item above on a scale of 0 to 10, ten being the most focus. *Please do not neglect this step.* This will not only help you accurately identify and understand the problems, it will provide you with many powerful solutions for what troubles you.

It is common for some individuals—after assessing themselves—to focus on higher numbers (e.g., 8, 9, 10), and to see this only as a negative, and to be discouraged. However, the reality is this: *The higher the number, the more opportunity there is for growth and blessings*

In addition, and as already mentioned, this helps us accurately diagnose *the cause* of our problems, while also directing us toward the remedy. Therefore, with the right perspective, the high numbers can and should actually give use lot of hope. Why? Because:

A High Number = A Big Opportunity

APPLICATION & DISCUSSION

+ Which areas are your biggest opportunities for you to grow in the most?

+ In what ways might you be encouraged by a high number attached to one or more of these?

+ What specifically did you learn about yourself, and what might need to change in your heart?

Possible Unforgiveness

+ In what ways do you struggle with resentment, anger, and re-living past offenses against you? Know that these are strong indicators of *a struggle with forgiveness*. With that in mind, who and what might you need to forgive?

It is very common for people, including wonderful Christians, to genuinely choose to forgive, yet not really achieve forgiveness. Why? Because they do not fully understand all that goes into forgiveness. For additional study, we have other helpful material available, including two books: *Forgiveness- A Practical And Biblical Handbook On How To Forgive* and *Forgiveness & Trust- Why Forgiving Someone Doesn't Mean You Have To Trust Them*

Possible Idols

As we delve into and assess our personal focus, it is not uncommon to stumble upon one or more idols in our lives. However, this, too, is *a huge opportunity for growth and freedom*. What, exactly, is an idol?

- An idol is something we assign far too much value to—especially when we give it more time, importance, and attention *than God—and* we *depend on* it for security, fulfillment, hope, peace of mind, comfort, and contentment, *rather than God* (cp. Ps 16:6; 106:36; 115; Jer 2:13; 17:5-8; Jon 2:8; Rom 1:25).

+ Did you detect any idols in your life from the previous list? If so, what are they (e.g., money; being in control; people and what they think of you; being perfect; marriage; job; porn; phone; your image)?

Sowing & Reaping

Always keep this principle in mind: *we reap what we sow*.

This is particularly important to remember when it comes to our hearts and our focus. Why, and how so? Even though God loves us as much as He does, if we focus on the things in the list above then we should *fully expect* to experience painful things, such as anxiety, insecurity, stress, hopelessness (i.e., depression), and for this to cause problems in our relationships. Even worse, we should also expect to lack joy, peace, hope, and security.

Nevertheless, many people seem to think that God's grace will somehow circumvent their unwise and harmful choices (Gal 6:7-8). As a result, they are not overly concerned about or motivated enough to change their hearts or their focus.

APPLICATION & DISCUSSION

+ In what ways, and to what degree do you tend to forget about the reaping-what-we-sow principle, especially when it comes to what occupies your mind and heart?

+ How might this play a part in your struggles with the stress, anxiety, etc. in your life?

This one thing—identifying the specific ways we focus on the wrong areas—can give us so much hope and help in understanding why we struggle the way we do. It also provides many solutions.

We Control Our Focus

This, then, gives us even more good news: *we are in control of what we focus on*. In addition, the less we focus on what we do not control—

and the more we rightly focus on what we do control—the better the fruit will be in our life (cp. Phil 4:4-9).

Living by this simple reality will give us an abundance of hope *and* other desired fruit as well. This also points to the many blessings we have in Jesus, and in living for Him, according to His Word:

- Through God and the power He gives us, *we can control what we focus on* (2 Cor 10:3-6; Lam 3:21; 2 Tim 1:7).

- What we focus on—and what occupies our hearts—largely determines the fruit in our lives (Is 26:3; Gal 5:22-23; Rom 8:5-6; Col 3:15-17; Ps 119:9, 165; Hab 3:17-19).

- There is no limit to the wonderful things we can set our minds on (Phil 4:4-9; Col 3:1-4)—therefore, there is no limit to the incredible fruit we can realize in our lives.

7

RIGHT FOCUS
BE RE-MINDED

... to be spiritually minded *is* **life** *and* **peace**.

— ROMANS 8:6

The Center for Bible Engagement (CBE) has done a great deal of research regarding how we focus on and engage in God's Word *and* the fruit this produces in our lives. Their conclusions give us some specific examples of positive outcomes from our engagement with the Word, as laid out below.

A key discovery from the CBE research is that the life of someone who engages scripture 4 or more times a week looks radically different from the life of someone who does not. In fact, the lives of Christians who do not engage the Bible most days of the week are statistically the same as the lives of non-believers.

Someone who engages the Bible 4 or more times a week is:

- 228% more likely to share faith with others
- 407% more likely to memorize scripture
- 59% less likely to view pornography
- 30% less likely to struggle with loneliness[1]

— BACK TO THE BIBLE (CBE)

Unsurprisingly, the difference maker here is *how often an individual engages with the Word of God*. More specifically, four or more times a week in the Word makes a massive difference in a person's life. On the other hand, less than four times produces essentially the same fruit as a person who does not know God, His love, His power, His grace, His forgiveness, His comfort, and His Word of life.

So, as we have seen, the more we engage our heart with the right things, the more we will experience much desired fruit, including true hope, joy, peace, freedom, love, and security. Even better, thanks to God and His Word, there is virtually no end to the many wonderful things with which we can fill our minds (e.g., Phil 4:8).

This, then, brings us to our list of things we would do well to focus on. These will inevitably produce good and godly fruit—to the extent our minds and hearts are occupied with them.

Good Things To Focus On

____ **God's Word** | Delighting in, meditating on, and putting our hope in *God's Word* (Ps 1:2-3; 19:7-11; 112:1; 119:15-16, 24, 35, 47-48, 70, 77-78, 92, 143; 130:5; 138:2; Josh 1:7-9; Col 3:16; Rom 15:4)

____ **God Himself** | Focusing on *God* (Is 26:3; Heb 3:1; 12:2ff; Col 3:1-4; Ps 37:4; 63:6; Lk 8:15)

____ **His Indwelling Word** | Letting the Word of Christ *dwell in us richly* throughout the day (Deut 6:6-7; Col 3:16)

____ **Prayer** | Rom 12:12; Phil 4:6-7; Col 4:2; 1 Thess 5:17

____ **God's Love For Us** | Ps 63:3; 1 Jn 3:16; 4:16; Rom 5:5, 8; 8:32; Jn 15:13; Matt 6:25ff

____ **Loving God** | Mk 12:30; Jn 14:15ff; 1 Jn 4:16; 5:3

____ **Loving others** | Mk 12:31; Acts 20:35; Phil 1:9-11; 1 Pet 4:8; Jas 5:19-20; 1 Jn 4:16

____ **This Day** | Focusing on *today*, and lovingly and faithfully fulfilling our responsibilities day-by-day (not taking on too much, too little, or worrying about tomorrow; Matt 6:25-34)

____ **Eternal Life** | Rom 6:23; 1 Cor 11:24-25; Col 1:12-14

____ **Rejoicing in the Lord** | Phil 4:4; 2 Cor 6:10; 1 Thess 5:16

____ **God's Works** | The amazing works of God (Ps 19:1ff; 77:12)

____ **Things "Above"** | Col 3:1-4; cp. Phil 3:18-21

____ **What is Unseen & Eternal** | 2 Cor 4:16; Matt 6:19-21; Heb 11:1

____ **Praising God** | 1 Chron 16:23-31; Ps 69:30; 75:1; 86:12

____ **Giving Thanks To God** | Practicing genuine gratitude in our hearts (Ps 35:18; Col 1:12; 2:7; 3:15-16; 4:2; 1 Thess 5:18; Heb 12:28; 13:15)

____ **Living In God's Grace** | Heb 4:16; 2 Cor 12:9-10; Jn 1:14, 17

____ **Nothing Is Wasted** | Remembering that whatever we do in the Lord *is not in vain* (1 Cor 15:58; Col 3:23-24)

____ **The New Covenant** | Learning about, remembering, and ruminating on the *New Covenant—and* being reminded that this is how God designed for us to live, love, and relate to Him, especially when it comes to our sin, weakness, failure, and suffering (e.g., 1 Cor 11:23-26; 2 Cor 3:5ff; 12:7-10; Gal 3:1ff; Heb 4:12-16); and remembering and rejoicing in the fact that—through His New Covenant—*we have all the love, value, and security we need in God alone.* This change in heart and focus is even more important for those who tend to live according to the Old Covenant (e.g., condemnation; guilt; performance-based mindset; perfectionism; fear-based; etc.)

____ **Truth** | Jn 17:17; 1 Cor 13:6; 2 Tim 2:15; 1 Jn 3:16

> Finally, brethren, *whatever things are* ***true***, whatever things are *noble*, whatever things are *just*, whatever things are *pure*, whatever things are *lovely*, whatever things are of *good report*, if there is any *virtue* and if there is anything *praiseworthy*—**meditate on these things.**
>
> — PHILIPPIANS 4:8

For a deeper understanding of your heart and focus, go back and rate your focus for each item on the previous list (on a scale of 0 to 10, ten being the most focus).

+ Out of the *19 Good Things To Focus On* which ones do you most desire to focus on more? Why those things?

This is worth stating again and again: our aim is not merely to think about the right things; our goal is to *consistently* meditate on—*and often wrestle with*—and work on *truly believing* these biblical truths. Why? *So that* our heart is strengthened in the Lord and His many blessings, such as His love, His power, His grace, His Word of truth, and a "sound mind."

> ... you welcomed it not as the word of men, *but as it is in truth, **the word of God, which also effectively works in you who believe**.*
>
> — 1 THESSALONIANS 2:13

> For God has not given us a spirit of fear, but of ***power*** and of ***love*** and of ***a sound mind***.
>
> — 2 TIMOTHY 1:7

When it comes to faith and belief, always remember that these things are not all-or-nothing. While a new believer goes from non-belief to believing, this also starts an ongoing *process of growing in belief*. We also know it will include several ups and downs. So, as we grow in faith—and in believing God, His Word of truth, and His promises—we will deepen our relationship with God. As a result, our security will grow, as will our joy and peace.

Perhaps we can all relate to the apostles, and to the dad talking to Jesus and this desire regarding belief.

> And the apostles said to the Lord, *"Increase our faith."*
>
> — LUKE 17:5

> Immediately the father of the child cried out [to Jesus] and said with tears, "Lord, I believe; *help my unbelief!*"
>
> — MARK 9:24

Focus & Hope

> *My soul, wait in silence for God only,*
> **For my hope is from Him.**
> *He only is my rock and my salvation,*
> *My stronghold; I shall not be shaken.*
> *On God my salvation and my glory rest;*
> *The rock of my strength, my refuge is in God.*
> *Trust in Him at all times, O people;*
> *Pour out your heart before Him;*
> *God is a refuge for us. Selah.*
>
> — PSALM 62:5-8 [NASB]

One way to understand our overall struggles and problems with focus is this: *our focus is tied to our hope*. What is more, our tendency is to put too much hope in the wrong things, and not in the right things (e.g., Jer 2:13; 17:5-9; Ps 1:1-3; Prov 3:5-6; 29:25; Rom 1:25).

To put it another way, the amount of hope or hopelessness in our life is largely determined by where, and in whom, we put our hope. Understanding this one thing will give us more opportunities to grow in hope, and to overcome many of our struggles. This vital truth is expounded on in many verses throughout God's Word.

> *Why are you cast down, O my soul?*
> *And why are you disquieted within me?*
> **Hope in God**; *For I shall yet praise Him,*
> *The help of my countenance and my God.*
>
> — PSALM 43:5

> **We wait in hope for the Lord;**
> *He is our help and our shield.*
> *In Him our hearts rejoice,*

for we trust in His holy name.
May your unfailing love rest upon us, O Lord,
even as we put our hope in You.

— PSALM 33:20-22 [NIV]

I wait for the Lord, my soul waits,
*And **in His word I do hope.***
My soul waits for the Lord
More than those who watch for the morning—
Yes, more than those who watch for the morning.

— PSALM 130:5-6

+ What might fruit in your life—good or bad—reveal about where you put your hope? Circle the things below that are true of you.

"I tend to put a large amount of my hope in ... "

- People, and what they think of me, and how they treat me
- My comfort
- My circumstances
- How well I compare to others
- The creation (rather than the Creator)
- My performance
- Money
- My career
- My appearance
- My health
- My intelligence and intellect
- My ability to control my circumstances
- What is "seen" and temporary
- What is "unseen" and eternal
- God, His Word of truth, and His love

> *Therefore we do not lose heart.* Though outwardly we are wasting away, yet inwardly we are being renewed day by day. For our light and momentary troubles are achieving for us an eternal glory that far outweighs them all. So we fix our eyes *not on what is seen, but on what is unseen.*
>
> **For what is seen is temporary, but what is unseen is eternal.**
>
> — 2 CORINTHIANS 4:16-18

To be clear, it is not wrong to put *some* hope in most of these. Who doesn't want good health? However, problems arise when we put *too much hope* in, and are overly focused on one or more of these things (e.g., our career; health; appearance; people).

On top of that, the biggest problem here occurs when we do not put nearly enough hope in God, His love, and His Word of truth. Yet this is exactly what we need to do. How much more when we are troubled in our hearts and lives?

> *In the multitude of my anxieties within me,*
> *Your comforts delight my soul.*
>
> — PSALM 94:19

> *Why are you cast down, O my soul?*
> *And why are you disquieted within me?*
> ***Hope in God;***
> *For I shall yet praise Him,*
> *The help of my countenance and my God.*
>
> — PSALM 42:11

APPLICATION & DISCUSSION

+ In light of the list above, what are the biggest opportunities for change and growth in your heart and where you put your hope?

+ Let's look at this another way, with a slightly different emphasis. What specific areas of life do you see as *never enough*? [For example: people affirming you and liking you; your performance; the performance of others; being secure in your salvation; money; having your needs met by others, especially your spouse; circumstances that go your way; having enough love; etc.]

+ What opportunities for growth might all this reveal about your focus, your beliefs, and the treasures of your heart?

We see in the verse below that the *"perfect* peace" everyone desires does not come from ideal circumstances or by just redirecting our attention away from undesirable things. Nor does it come from merely focusing on God.

Such peace comes by *truly trusting the person of God*, and this trust is greatly enhanced by knowing Him and His character. This, then, enables us to keep our mind "stayed" on God, and on His trustworthy love, which results in the overall desired fruit, keeping us "in perfect peace." Could anything be more desirable than that?

> *You will keep him* **in perfect peace,**
> *Whose mind is stayed on You,*
> **Because he trusts in You.**
>
> — ISAIAH 26:3

8

DISTRACTED FOCUS

DRAWN AWAY FROM THE MAIN THINGS

> Now it happened as they went that He entered a certain village; and a certain woman named Martha welcomed Him into her house. And she had a sister called Mary, **who also sat at Jesus' feet and heard His word.** But Martha was **distracted** with much serving, and she approached Him and said, "Lord, do You not care that my sister has left me to serve alone? Therefore tell her to help me." And Jesus answered and said to her, "Martha, Martha, **you are worried and troubled about many things. But one thing is needed**, and **Mary has chosen that good part**, which will not be taken away from her."
>
> — LUKE 10:38-42

One of the worst aviation disasters in U.S. history occurred in December of 1972 when Eastern Airlines Flight 401 crashed into the Florida Everglades, about 18 miles from the airport. Tragically, 101 individuals died. However, 75 people miraculously survived.

Re-Minded

Why did the plane crash? Did it run out of fuel? Was there a storm? Were they hijacked? Did a wing fall off? Was there evil intent from the pilots or others?

No. Nothing like that happened. At the core of this major catastrophe was actually a very small problem, at least seemingly, which was this: The flight crew became *distracted.*

More specifically, they became *over-occupied* by a malfunctioning lightbulb that was connected to the landing gear. However, in the bigger picture—and as a result of this distraction—the pilots grew oblivious to what was most vital in that moment: They were steadily descending toward the earth, as they unwittingly stopped flying the plane.

Worst of all, because of their faulty focus—which distracted them from the single most important thing—they slammed into the ground, killing over one hundred people. As stated in the NTSB report: "*Preoccupation* with a malfunction of the nose landing gear position indicating system *distracted* the crew's attention from the instruments and *allowed the descent to go unnoticed*" (emphasis added).

Was that light important? Yes, absolutely. It indicated the status of their landing gear, which was, of course, essential to their safe arrival (the gear was fine, it was just the lightbulb that was the problem). However, because of a simple malfunction, they were *drawn away* from their main job: actually flying the plane.

As terrible as it was, there were some good things to come out of the tragedy, at least for others. Most importantly, this particular crash led to the FAA learning from the pilots' mistakes and, therefore, making critical changes to help limit future deadly distractions in the cockpit, especially when taking off and landing.

There are many valuable things we, too, can learn from their faulty focus. The first of which is just how incredibly important our focus is to our wellbeing, *and* that of others. The second one is also a central

Re-Minded

topic of this chapter: that is, the things we focus on do not have to be *bad* in order to cause trouble and harm.

For example, a lot of damage can and does happen simply by being "*distracted*" from the main thing, or from other good things. Martha learned several painful lessons about this as well. [Please make sure you take ample time to read and process the five verses above (Lk 10:38-42), as we will be doing a *deep* dive into this section of Scripture.]

In fact, it is vital that we gain a deeper understanding of that word "distracted" (in verse 40), which is also translated as "cumbered." It is understood as: "to draw around, **to draw away**, distract," "**to be driven about mentally**" and "**to be over-occupied**, *too busy*, about a thing."

This one word, by itself—and the meanings of this word—help explain why so many people are so troubled, and seek out counseling (e.g., they are "driven about mentally," "over-occupied," etc.). In other words, a great deal of damage is often caused—including "*mentally*" —when we are distracted, over-burdened, and drawn away from what is right, true, best, and what is of utmost importance. This usually occurs when we are *too busy*, or because our mind is "*over-occupied*." [The NTSB report on the 1972 plane crash used the word "preoccupation."]

Therefore, always keep this in mind: certain troubles in life can and will happen when our focus is on something neutral, or even good, *but* not on what is truly "needed," or on what is more important at the time.

+ In what ways does any of this resonate regarding yourself or a loved one?

Unfortunately, there are several more possible complications that come from being distracted. For example, many who are over-busy are not only drawn away from the right things, they often do not realize the reality of their plight, similar to those pilots.

In addition, there are those who are aware of being overloaded, yet they see this harmful and stressful state as a good thing. Why? For two main reasons: first, taking on too much can appeal to our pride and sinful nature, *and* secondly, we are often motivated to do this out of *the fear of man*, (i.e., worrying about what people think of us—and needing their approval, while fearing their disproval).

Adding another layer of difficulty here, many over-occupied individuals frequently compare the amount of work they do to that of others (cp. Lk 18:11-12). This is usually revealed in their anger, envy, resentment, harsh judgments, false accusations, an adversarial attitude, and even rage (e.g., Martha vs Mary; Martha vs Jesus).

On an individual level, the more a person walks in these ways, the more he or she will become anxious, stressed, and depressed. Some might even struggle with suicidal ideation. What is more, so much of this very thing (being drawn away; driven about mentally; over-occupied) is at the heart of what is frequently referred to today as a mental health crisis. While this society-wide struggle is very real, fortunately, *so are the solutions*, many of which are laid out in this section, and throughout the rest of the book.

Martha, Martha ...

To Martha's credit, she clearly had a desire to serve. However, what was the specific fruit produced by her faulty focus, over-busyness, and disjointed priorities? We can observe many painful things in Luke's account.

- Sinful anger
- Spike in stress and anxiety
- Being overwhelmed
- Resentment
- Rage

- Doubting God

- Doubting His love and care for her

- Being angry with God

- Missing out on a perfect opportunity *to be with Jesus*

- Missing out on the blessings and truth of God's Word

- Missing out on amazing fellowship, including with *the apostles and future leaders of the Church*

- Missing out on what was truly needed

- Missing out on joy, hope, love, and peace.

Can all of these bad things happen when we have good intentions? Yes, absolutely. In fact, this helps us understand why so many wonderful and well-intentioned people struggle so much.

It is also helps us to see how easy it is to deceive ourselves here, for example: "Yeah, but I was trying to help and bless others … and I was just focused on what had to be done." However, no matter the intent of our heart, these painful outcomes will certainly happen whenever we are distracted, over-burdened, focused on the wrong things, and have lost sight of the most important things (cp. Mk 4:19).

Making this even more troublesome, Martha's escalating stress increasingly intensified her emotions, as can be the case for all of us. She then took her anger out—not on her enemies—but on those she loved the most, which also damaged these invaluable relationships. This not only included her sister—who, in contrast, *chose* the "good part"—but God Himself. In fact, Jesus took the brunt of Martha's blowup.

Over all of this we see that Martha was *"troubled"* by many things. It is vital that we understand the Greek word here, as it means: "to be troubled *in mind.*" That word comes from another Greek word "týrbē," which means a "tumult" or a "riot." The understanding from these words gives us a good sense of what was going on in Martha's mind, and what often happens in the minds of billions of people today.

This also explains why Jesus encouraged and directed her—and you and me—to do this: *As much as it is possible—no matter what you have going on—always prioritize, focus on, and enjoy what is truly needed, which is God and His Word.*

We will avoid so many problems in life—and realize so many blessings—when we faithfully follow our Lord's direction here. However, and as you likely know, there are always things that compete with our time with God and God's Word. The competition here includes good things and not so good things (Mk 4:19).

Nevertheless, it is still up to us to choose to navigate these challenges in the right ways. And the fruit in our life—both current and longterm—will reveal the quality of our choices, and the treasures of our hearts, *especially in connection to God's Word.*

> Still others, like seed sown among thorns, *hear the word; but the worries of this life, the deceitfulness of wealth and **the desires for other things come in and choke the word, making it unfruitful**.* Others, like seed sown on good soil, *hear the word, accept it, **and produce a crop—thirty, sixty or even a hundred times what was sown**.*
>
> — MARK 4:18-20

This is one reason why Jesus Himself praises Mary and her choice in the midst of a potentially distracting situation: "Mary has *chosen* that good part, which will not be taken away from her." [Notice the potential here to be *re-minded*—not just for Martha, but for all of us.]

However, when it comes to Martha, if we use more modern descriptions of what happened, some people might say she spiraled, had a panic attack, was overtaken by her emotions, had a meltdown, or even a mental breakdown. And we all know that a breakdown will always happen whenever there is an overload. Thankfully, Jesus gave her (and us) the remedy.

Take note how these two things, by themselves—being "driven about mentally" and "troubled in mind"—explain so much of what is behind the many struggles in today's society. This is particularly true with what is commonly described as mental health struggles.

What is more, notice how God and His Word not only get to the heart of these problems, but how He also abundantly provides many solutions (e.g., Matt 11:28-30; Phil 4:4-8; Rom 12:2; Rom 8:5ff; Is 26:3; Lam 3:21ff). Tragically, these divine remedies are often neglected, scoffed at, and even rejected—not just by unbelievers, but by countless people who claim Christ.

APPLICATION & DISCUSSION

+ What would happen to the "mental health crisis" if everyone somehow eliminated all aspects of being "driven about mentally" and "troubled in mind," as described in these verses?

+ What does that tell us about some of the causes and solutions to this society-wide problem?

+ In what specific ways can the Church help in this?

Negative Narratives

Another invaluable insight here is this: it is common in similar scenarios for there to be *a destructive and self-deceiving narrative* going on in our mind. When it comes to Martha's situation, some possible negative notions running through her mind are: "This is so unfair!" "Why am I stuck here doing all the work?" "Where's my silly sister?" "She *always* does this to me." "Why do *I* always have to sacrifice so much?" "I am so under-appreciated?" "Why am I the only one working?!" "Nobody cares about me!" "No matter how much I do, it is never enough." "Why isn't anyone coming to help?! Can't they see how much I have to do here? Don't they hear me banging the pots and pans and slamming cabinet doors?" "Doesn't Jesus see what is going on? I guess He doesn't care." "Why won't He solve my problem?" "Because I have been so unfairly treated, I have a right to blow up on others." "My angry outburst is more than justified!"

+ In what ways, and to what degree do any of these resonate with you, or in relationships with others?

For a better understanding, here are some general rules regarding negative narratives: the more we feed these faulty ideas in our head, the more we will be angry, stressed, overly emotional, hopeless, driven by our emotions, enraged, and "troubled in mind." And, in turn, the less objective and less rational we will be. This, then, will likely lead to erroneous judgments and false accusations—which means we will sin against and hurt others, causing damage to our relationship with them, as well as our relationship with God.

Can all of this carnage occur merely by feeding a negative narrative in our mind? Yes, absolutely. In fact, this is one of the most destructive under-the-radar things we can do to ourselves, with the damage often overflowing into our relationships as well.

However, there is great news. We can *all* be *re-minded*. More specifically, we can learn how to stop these lies, while changing the focus of our hearts, which will then prevent these harmful things from happening. And we can do this by calling to mind the right things, while replacing the negative narratives with the truth. This, then, will produce wonderful fruit in our life (e.g., Lam 3:21; 2 Cor 3:5).

Task-Focused & Faulty Needs

We also see that Martha was over-focused on the *tasks* at hand. She took on far more than she could chew (pardon the pun). However, in so doing, she was *distracted* from the main thing—from the one thing that was truly needed, and from what was more important than the tasks (e.g., people, and how she treated them; pleasing God).

Completing tasks and serving others obviously has value. However, the *one thing* that was actually needed here was *far* more valuable than what Martha chose to focus on as her priority or need. Here are some examples of her possible *faulty needs*: needing to make an incredible meal for everyone; needing to get her house perfectly clean for her company; needing approval from others, while fearing their disapproval.

All of this helps clarify a couple of pivotal principles regarding needs:

- Neglecting our true and superlative need—while also making non-needs into pressing needs—explains so many struggles in our life, and in our relationships.

- Ever-growing discernment, wisdom, and self-discipline will go a long way in helping us overcome our struggles with faulty needs, and in faithfully fulfilling our true needs.

APPLICATION & DISCUSSION

+ In what ways do you struggle in this area, particularly by making non-needs into "needs"? Do any specific non-needs come to mind?

+ In what ways do you make tasks more important than people—especially when it comes to how you treat them and value them?

+ In what ways do you make tasks more important than spending quality time with God and His Word?

Here is another compounding factor with Martha's focus-problem: She was over-focused on perceived or exaggerated slights and injustices—which were connected to her false needs and wrong priorities. This faulty focus resulted in pouring more and more fuel on the fire inside of her. And, in turn, this eventually culminated in her explosion, the damage she did to herself and others, as well as her relationships, including her relationship with God.

+ From what you have read so far about Martha, which fruit and actions of hers resonate with you the most, if any?

After considering Martha's plight, do you see how sneaky-destructive it is when we focus *too much* on something, even a good thing? How much more harmful is it when we are "drawn away" from the "one thing" that is truly "needed"?

While Martha's behavior may have been good *outwardly* (serving), at least initially, this is misleading, if not fully self-deceiving. Why? Because *inwardly* her focus, priorities, and the treasures of her heart were off the mark. She also seemed to live by a performance-based mindset (i.e., trying to find her value and identity in her performance), rather than grace and truth (i.e., the New Covenant, finding her worth and identity in God; cp. Gal 3:1ff; 5:1ff).

+ In what ways have you been misled by your good behavior or intentions, while having a faulty priority or focus?

The One Thing

In contrast to Martha, Mary had it right. How so? In the midst of all the busyness, social interactions, and potential distractions, Mary made the right choice. In other words, she *chose* to prioritize what was most important and needed. What, exactly, was this *"one thing"*? It was *being with Jesus, and listening to and learning from His Word*.

Now, that might seem to be a simple and easy thing to do—maybe even *too* easy. However, it can actually be exceedingly challenging for many of us, particularly when we have other things competing for our time and attention (cp. Mk 4:19).

In fact, one of the biggest determining factors in one's life is how well they establish and live out the right priorities (e.g., Matt 6:19-34). Yet these will often be put to the test, particularly when we have many valuable things happening at the same time. This was the dilemma that occurred for both Mary and Martha; yet they each made very different choices.

Nevertheless, a common objection here goes something like this: "Yeah, but ... there were things that *had to be done*. Martha focused on those, and Mary did not. Therefore, Martha was right, and Mary was wrong!"

Yes, there were, in fact, very real responsibilities at hand, *but that is the point*. How so? Because this is generally true for all of us. We will always have things we need to do, and many important things going on at the same time, such as: children; spouse; work; school; God; God's Word; prayer; church; ministry, family; friends; girlfriend or boyfriend; serving; eating; exercise; tasks/chores.

However, we all choose to approach things differently—which reveals a lot about us, especially the treasures of our hearts (cp. Deut 30:14-20; Ps 84:10; Matt 6:19-21; Lk 6:45; Gal 5:1-26). What is more, the decisions we make here have great power to alter the trajectory of our lives—in good ways, and in not so good ways.

More importantly, whatever we choose to do, including good things like serving, it is essential that we do these with the right motives and priorities (Matt 6:1ff; Col 3:24-25). This, will always lead to personal blessings, like joy and peace. On the other hand, doing things that are good—yet having a poor attitude, the wrong priorities, or less-than stellar motives—will always lead to bad fruit, including anger, blow-ups, complaining, despair, resentment, and worse.

What largely makes the difference here comes through *the treasures of our hearts*—and choosing to focus on and prioritize *who* and what is most important—all while trusting God with all of the above. This includes the times when certain tasks are not fully completed—or not finished in the preferred manner or timeframe (cp. Matt 6:19-21, 25-34; 2 Tim 1:12; Prov 3:5-6; 1 Pet 5:7).

All or Nothing Thinking

This brings up a common yet trouble-causing mindset by which we get tripped up, which is *all-or-nothing thinking*. Some examples of this all-or-nothing mindset include: either everything comes out great, or I have failed; either I make everyone happy, or I am a failure; either I have finished all my tasks, or, if not, I have completely failed; either I am firmly walking with God, or, if I blow it in just one area, then I am a horrible Christian, and God probably does not love me anymore.

+ Does any of that resonate with you?

It is very possible Martha struggled with all-or-nothing thinking, at least in one way or another. For example, she might have falsely assumed her choice was: "Either I make an amazing meal, one with all my special dishes, and with a perfectly clean house, while I run around serving everyone, *or* I drop all of that, no one gets *any* food or drinks, and I sit down with Jesus ... *but* people will think I am a horrible host." Usually that last part is the core issue and heart problem with all-or-nothing thinking, which is: *what people might think about us* (i.e., the fear of man; Prov 29:25).

However, this situation was not an all-or-nothing matter. There were other choices Martha could have made, like choosing to whip up a few snacks, as opposed to a full meal—while not worrying about what people might think of her. If she did this, then Martha would have freed herself up for the *one thing* that was needed. As a result, she would have had ample time with her Lord, and not thrown her sister under the bus. Best of all, she would have had an incredibly blessed day with Jesus and others. In addition, it is possible that Martha could have asked for help, or even delegated some responsibilities, rather than take on everything.

Of course, we will never know all of the dynamics in that moment, but if Martha was ensnared in all-or-nothing thinking—which is familiar to many of us—then this could explain a lot of what happened in her mind and in her home.

+ In what ways might *all-or-nothing thinking* impact your mind, home, work, school, relationships, and the fruit in your life?

To Mary's credit, in the midst of the many things going on, she was not distracted from *the one thing* that is *truly needed*. What is that universal superlative need? It is Jesus, God's Word, and our relationship with Him. In other words, it is prioritizing quality time with God and His Word, all with the right heart. David, the man after God's own heart, was certainly in agreement with this "one thing."

> ***One thing*** *I ask of the Lord,*
> *this is what I seek:*
> *that I may dwell in the house of the Lord*
> *all the days of my life,*
> *to gaze upon the beauty of the Lord*
> *and to seek him in his temple.*
>
> — PSALM 27:4 [NIV]

George Muller

Few people in history were busier than the great George Muller. Perhaps no one had as many vital responsibilities as he did.

- He was a full-time pastor (this, by itself, includes numerous responsibilities)
- He preached *three times a week*, and over 10,000 times in his lifetime
- He read the Bible all the way through well over 200 times
- He personally answered hundreds, if not thousands, of letters by hand
- He established over 117 schools which educated over 120,000 individuals
- He established and ran a ministry called *The Scripture Knowledge Institution*, which spread the gospel and God's Word to an unknown number of people (although it is known that he gave away over 250,000 Bibles)

- He established and built several orphanages, all in the midst of great poverty and great need, by relying fully on God, through much prayer
- He hired, supervised, and cared for a large number of staff members
- He fed and oversaw the care of thousands of orphans over several decades
- He raised and was responsible for over $150,000,000 (in today's currency)
- He traveled all over the world to share God's Word (to 42 countries, on five continents, traveling 200,000 miles, all before the invention of the airplane)
- Making things even more incredible, he did not take a salary for the last 68 years of his ministry

Given Muller's astonishing busyness, it makes everything above even more impressive as we see, from his own words, how he was in full harmony with the "one thing" spoken of by David and Jesus.

> The primary business I must attend to every day is to fellowship with the Lord. The first concern is not how much I might serve the Lord, but how my inner man might be nourished.[1]
>
> — GEORGE MULLER

> But in what way shall we attain to this settled happiness of soul? How shall we learn to enjoy God? How obtain such an all-sufficient soul-satisfying portion in him as shall enable us to let go the things of this world as vain and worthless in comparison? I answer, This happiness is to be obtained through the study of the Holy Scriptures. God has therein revealed Himself unto us in the face of Jesus Christ.[2]
>
> — GEORGE MULLER

Even with his staggering amount of responsibilities, *Muller daily chose the right priorities*. That was the "secret" to his fruitfulness. It is clear that, in the midst of so many moving parts of his life, he faithfully followed through on his commitment to the one thing that was truly needed: *time with God, time in prayer, and time in His Word*.

Put another way, Muller's success was not in how much he took on. Rather, it was his relationship with God, nourishing his "inner man," his faithfulness to the right priorities, and trusting God with the outcome of his activities.

However, many, if not most believers generally take the opposite approach. We largely focus on our busyness, while neglecting what is truly needed and of utmost value: a loving and faithful relationship with God—which includes much prayer and time in His Word—which feeds and strengthens our soul, which empowers us for all that God entrusts to us.

Compounding this problem, we often make excuses for our neglect of what matters most, such as: "I'm just too busy," or, "I have had a lot going on recently." Even when that is true—and it often is—our busyness does not explain or justify our choices, particularly when it comes to not *making the main thing the main thing*. In contrast, Mary chose "the good part"—the one thing that was truly needed—and she was extremely blessed as a result.

APPLICATION & DISCUSSION

+ What are some things you can learn and apply from George Muller's faith, faithfulness, and priorities?

+ What would you tell your future self if a month from now you gave the excuse: "I'm just too busy for _____" (e.g., time with God and His Word; time with my kids, spouse, etc.)?

> *But Martha was* distracted *with much serving ...*
>
> — LUKE 10:40

Destructive Distractions

Here is a modern day conundrum to illustrate how we are distracted from the one thing. It is very common for believers—including mature Christians—to spend far less time with God and His Word *while on vacation*. The point here is that, while we have *far more free time*, we often spend *less time* in the Word, and in prayer. But why is that? It seems the opposite would be true.

While time is always a factor—and having more time always helps—time is actually not the main issue. Rather, it comes back to our hearts, to self-discipline, and to our priorities, choices, and the treasures of our hearts. Thankfully, with God empowering us, and giving us everything we need, we can change and grow in all of these areas.

With all this in mind, the following list contains several things which might not be bad in and of themselves—however, there is definitely evil in much of these. The main concern here is *when we give too much time and attention* to them, which results in us being distracted and, therefore, negatively impacted (cp. Mk 4:19).

Not only can these things draw us away from what is best, but also from what is truly needed. In addition, they often cause us to be "troubled in mind," and lead to a great deal of damage in our relationships. And, of course, we can make it even worse when we indulge in the bad parts, such as the harmful content in music, movies, social media, the internet, etc.

+ While most things on this list do have some value, which of these do you give too much of your time and focus?

Things That Occupy Your Time & Focus

    Your phone (or other devices)

    Your performance

    Your appearance

    Social media

    Intellectual knowledge (head knowledge that does not really *impact our heart*, nor help others)

    Your rights—and what you deserve (real or perceived; cp. Jonah 4)

    Solving problems (ruminating on various issues that need to be resolved)

    The news (and politics, and political news)

    Music (this likely has the most *underrated harmful impact* on our minds and hearts)

    TV/Movies/Entertainment

    Video games (and other games)

    Relationships (or *potential* relationships)

    Money and material possessions (cp. 1 Tim 6:6-10)

    Sports or hobbies

    Job/career, working, studying, exercising, "serving" (e.g., Lk 10:40)

    Ministry

    Daydreaming, thought life

    Your feelings

If you dwell on your own feelings about things rather than dwelling on the faithfulness, the love, and the mercy of God, then you're likely to have a terrible, horrible, no good, very bad day. Our feelings are very fleeting and ephemeral, aren't they? We can't depend on them for five minutes at a time. But dwelling on the love, faithfulness, and mercy of God is always safe.[3]

— ELISABETH ELLIOT

APPLICATION & DISCUSSION

For a deeper understanding of your heart and focus, take some time and rate yourself for each item above: 0 being a healthy focus, and 10 being the most damaging and distracting over-focus. Always keep in mind this reality: *the higher the number, the better the opportunity for growth and blessings.*

+ Which areas are your biggest opportunities where you can and need to grow the most?

+ In what ways are you similar to *Mary*?

+ Which aspects of *Martha* do you see in your life? [For example: over-occupied; "driven about mentally," at least at times; stressed out; distracted, especially from prioritizing time with God and His Word; feeding negative narratives in your mind; resentment; angry blow-ups, particularly toward those closest to you; lacking joy, security, and peace of mind; focusing more on tasks than on people and how you treat them]

\+ What are some specific things you can and need to do to change these things?

\+ When it comes to any Martha-like traits in you, in what ways have these hurt those around you and caused damage in your relationships?

\+ Detecting patterns can be a powerful way to grow. Therefore, to isolate the areas you can grow in the most, finish the following sentences that apply to you:

- I am often overly-busy and "over-occupied" in the areas of:

- I am "driven about mentally" when:

- I experience the most stress when:

- The things that distract me the most from time with God and His Word are:

- The things that distract me the most overall are:

- When it comes to disjointed priorities, the excuses I rely on the most are:

- The three most common negative narratives I struggle with are:

+ From the previous sentences, what did you learn about the specific areas you need to grow in the most?

+ If being over-occupied and troubled in mind for ten minutes will cause a great deal of problems, what will a person's life look like if he or she is *frequently* over-occupied, "driven about mentally," and troubled in their mind?

+ How might this overall biblical understanding both explain *and* help remedy many common struggles with what is referred to today as *mental health*?

Are you over-occupied, have too much on your plate, and distracted from the things that are much more important and needed? To the degree these are true of you, you should fully expect to be "troubled in mind," and to struggle with stress, anxiety, and eventually depression. While these experiences are never pleasant, we can learn to use them in a very constructive way, as God intended.

When you are troubled in your mind—and, therefore, likely experience anxiety, stress, rage, or possibly depression—this is a warning that you are probably over-busy, over-burdened, and that the focus of your heart is off (Mk 4:19; Rom 8:5-6). God actually designed us to function in this way. These are your built-in cues and motivations to be *re-minded*, particularly by making the appropriate changes in your heart and mind. We will expound on God's design much more in another chapter.

+ What are your most important takeaways from all of the above about Martha, Mary, and being distracted in your focus?

9

IDOLS

UNDERSTAND & OVERCOME THEM

> *For My people have committed two evils:*
> **They have forsaken Me,**
> **the fountain of living waters,**
> *And hewn themselves cisterns*—broken
> cisterns that can hold no water.
>
> — JEREMIAH 2:13

Remember that an idol is something that we give too much importance to—and which competes with God—and has become more important than God. An idol can also be something that we make more important than other things which are of greater value, such as our spouse, kids, friends, the truth, or doing what is right and loving.

Keep in mind, however, that an idol is not all-or-nothing. It is often a matter of degree. This means we can have a major idol, a minor one, or somewhere in between (e.g., "1 to 10").

In addition, when it comes to modern phraseology, some idols are often labeled as "addictions." But whatever we call them, if we are to truly overcome these things, we must have the right understanding of what they actually are, and how they function: they are deceptive and destructive *dependencies*.

> **IDOLS:** In addition to neglecting and offending God, an idol has three main things at its core: *a harmful dependency, self-deception*, and a *false need* driving the ongoing damage. These, in turn, distract us and draw us away from three life-giving, life-determining realities: *our dependency on God, our true needs*, and *our sufficiency in Him*. Those last three truths are also the very solutions to idolatry, to destructive dependencies/addictions, and to all sorts of other problems in life (e.g., Jer 2:13; 17:5-8; Rom 1:25; Is 44:15-20; cp. Ps 115; Lk 10:38-42).

> They *exchanged the truth of God for a lie,* **and worshiped and served created things rather than the Creator**—who is forever praised. Amen.
>
> — ROMANS 1:25 [NIV]

Whether the idol/addiction is big or small, here is how these dependencies *functionally* play out: we usually start by subtly and gradually "exchang(ing) the truth of God for a lie." As a result, *we increasingly depend on* one or more aspects of the creation, rather than the "Creator." And we do this usually for the purpose of obtaining desired feelings—often through instant gratification—and/or to escape unwanted thoughts and feelings.

Therefore, instead of living according to "the truth of God"—and rather than going to and relying on the Lord for help, comfort, security, hope, strength, relief, truth, love, grace, peace, joy, and blessings —we give our attention, time, energy, emotion, and money to an idol. In other words, we depend on something in *the creation* rather than *the Creator*. Why? Because we believe doing so will give us some level of happiness, security, relief, and peace. However, all of that is a huge "lie."

What is more, this lie always fails, of course. Not only that, this approach will always cause damage and further deceive us. Worse, we delude ourselves by thinking we are in control of the idol. Yet, in reality, the opposite is happening. We are increasingly surrendering control of our lives over to the idol.

But it gets even worse. The more we depend on the idol, the more power it has over us—and, in turn, the less freedom, security, control, and peace we will have. While this idol will certainly give us some good feelings (e.g., pleasure, usually through immediate gratification), these feelings are *always fleeting*. This, then, deepens both the deception and the dependency.

The reality is, an idol can never, ever truly satisfy us. And whatever it might give, it is never enough. Therefore, even if we feel good for a little while, we soon need more.

This, at least in extreme situations, sets us up for a crippling and life-dominating dependency. Not only that, we are depending on a lie—one which can never deliver what we truly need.

However, when we are under the bondage of idolatry, we continually depend on the idol, in the hope that it will meet our need, something it can never do. No wonder the addictive life is so increasingly maddening and destructive.

Furthermore, in the ever-elusive pursuit of lasting security and peace —which the idol failed to give, and *cannot* give—we continue to go back to the very thing which has failed every single time. Worst of all, and revealing the very heart of the matter, we continue to depend on what is broken and "does not satisfy," rather than going to the one and only Source who can truly satisfy us.

In big or small ways, this cycle of torment is repeated, often daily, and sometimes multiple times a day—leading to more and more deception, hopelessness, and tyranny. Worst of all, this destructive dependency also keeps us away from the real solutions.

Thankfully, we have a God who will not only truly and fully satisfy us—He *longs* to do so (Is 30:18; Matt 11:28-30; Rom 5:5, 8; 8:32; Heb 4:16). Better yet, He will freely give us exactly what we truly need. However, this does require something on our part—namely, that we repent, utterly forsake our idol and, instead, increasingly believe and put our hope in Him.

> *Those who cling to worthless idols*
> *forfeit the grace that could be theirs.*
>
> — JONAH 2:8 [NIV]

> *Ho! Everyone who thirsts,*
> *Come to the waters;*
> *And you who have no money,*
> *Come, buy and eat.*
> *Yes, come, buy wine and milk*
> Without money *and* without price.
> **Why do you spend money for what is not bread,**
> **And your wages for what does not satisfy?**
> *Listen carefully to Me, and eat what is good,*
> **And let your soul delight itself in abundance.**
> Incline your ear, and come to Me.
> Hear, and **your soul shall live;**
>
> — ISAIAH 55:1-3

Making this overall problem much worse, the Church has developed a serious dependency problem of its own. How so? In the hope of helping people overcome their individual struggles, particularly with destructive dependencies, rather than firmly depending on God and His Word—and the countless life-transforming truths therein—much of the Church depends on the world's wisdom (cp. Col 2:8; Ps 1:1-3; 2 Tim 3:16-17; 2 Pet 1:3-4; 1 Jn 4:5-6).

At best, these methodologies merely shift the harmful dependency onto another aspect of the creation (e.g., man's wisdom; programs; people). Worse, these struggling individuals are not directed to sufficiently depend on the one and only true God, and His power and perfect Word of life—which is the only way to truly be set free (e.g., Ps 19:7-11; Jn 8:31ff; 14:6; 2 Cor 3:17; Gal 5:1ff). [For more, we have additional material available on the biblical understanding of addictions.]

APPLICATION & DISCUSSION

+ Are there things from the previous list of distractions (e.g., phone) that you are giving too much time, energy, thought life, and even money towards that may indicate it is becoming an idol?

+ Which of these are you frequently depending on *for the purpose of escaping unwanted thoughts or feelings*?

+ In what ways does your time and interaction with your phone (or similar device) take up too much of your time, distract you, generate stress and anxiety, and hinder you and draw you away from the right things (e.g., going to bed on time; spending time with God, His Word, key people, or your overall responsibilities)?

Not surprisingly, the over-focus on our phone is often the number one distraction, by far, for most people—as well as the things associated with phones, like social media, videos, games, work. Therefore, the so-called "smart" phone represents one of the most common idols in today's world.

Another major concern that needs to be discussed: it is common for people to be very unaware of how much of their time and energy is spent on their phone, and how this negatively impacts them, their relationships, and their efficiency and productivity in other areas of life (e.g., work; school).

+ In whatever way you assess yourself, please also ask those who know and love you about your phone usage. What do they say?

+ How does your phone usage inhibit, weaken, or harm the important relationships in your life?

+ To what degree does this distract you from your main responsibilities (e.g., work; studying)?

+ To what degree would you label your phone an idol in your life (on a scale from 0 to 10?

+ What are some specific and tangible changes you can make in this area?

Practical Changes

When it comes to addressing phone or technology usage, here are several helpful examples of practical changes you can make:

- Intentionally plug in your phone on the other side of the room at night, or in another room (out of reach or sight)
- Turn off all devices during certain times of the day
- Set your devices to a finite amount of time they can be used
- Delete certain apps
- Work with others for accountability in this specific area
- Cut off most, if not all, social media—or at least make sure you are using these for beneficial purposes (e.g., work; to encourage others; ministry; etc.).

In addition, try not to be on your phone in the following situations: when you are in the company of others; in any direct conversation with one or more people; at school; at work; at church or Bible study; eating a meal with others; while doing other activities (e.g., playing a game; watching TV or a movie). Not only is this rude, it often reveals a lack of value that you have for others—and negatively impacts you as well.

What is more, while we might think we are multitasking when we use our phone while doing something else, this often ends up dividing our attention, at best. Worse, it usually distracts us and draws us away from what should be valued more, kind of like Martha. It also hinders our general ability to focus.

Self-Discipline

Over all of this, and better yet, work on your *self-discipline*. This, too, involves a dependency on God and a change in our heart. It also includes the ability to make the right, but often difficult, choices, like saying "no" to certain things. And it requires the wisdom and decisiveness to lessen or cut out unhelpful or harmful things in our life.

While most of us likely do not realize it, much of our life is heavily impacted by how self-disciplined we are—particularly in key areas, such as: love; our focus; studying; eating; work; relationships; our walk with God; exercise; spending habits. What is more, to the degree we lack self-discipline, we are inviting danger in to our lives, as Scripture point out.

> *Like a city whose walls are broken down*
> *is a man who lacks self-control.*
>
> — PROVERBS 25:28 [NIV]

What, exactly, is self-discipline? And how can it be understood? Functionally, self-discipline is making decisions in life based on what we *know* is true, best, right, necessary, and loving—and *not* on what we *want or feel* (cp. 2 Tim 1:7; Ti 1:8; 2:11-14). In other words, when it comes to how we live, and how we make choices, *what we **know** is right always trumps what we **feel** in the moment.*

For example, there are times when we may not feel like going to work or school—or praying, reading our Bible, exercising, or being kind and loving. However, through faith, wisdom, and self-discipline, we will not do what we *feel* like doing in those moments. Rather, we will follow through on what we know is best, right, and loving. Better yet, at some point we will be very glad we chose to do what we knew was best. On the other hand, if we choose to follow our feelings then we will often soon regret it.

In the meantime, while we are growing in self-discipline and faith, we may need to implement one or more of the above examples, such as restrictions on our phone, etc. In addition, we all need help sometimes. If and when this occurs in your life, please seek someone who is biblically qualified to come alongside you to help overcome struggles—all while strengthening your heart and relationship with Jesus.

+ How would you describe your functional self-discipline in at least one or two sentences?

+ In which areas are you the most self-disciplined, and which ones need the most improvement (phone, work, praying, studying, spending, time-management, loving others with the truth, your relationship with God, etc.)?

10

OUR FRUIT

A WINDOW TO OUR SOUL

> The lamp of the body is the eye. If therefore your eye is good, your whole body will be full of light. But if your eye is bad, your whole body will be full of darkness. If therefore the light that is in you is darkness, how great is that darkness!
>
> — MATTHEW 6:22-23

Perhaps you have heard Shakespeare's famous line, "The eyes are the window to your soul." While some believe he drew this idea from the Scripture above, these verses are not about what others might see in our eyes. Rather, they are more about what we choose to let into our minds and hearts, through what we focus on—which then largely results in the fruit we produce.

Is there some truth in Shakespeare's declaration? Yes. In fact, there are many things that can help us see more clearly into our hearts, through which we can learn more about ourselves and others. Some examples include our body language (Neh 2:2), our responses to difficulties (Deut 8:2), the words we say (cp. Lk 6:45), and how we respond to correction. However, a much more accurate way of gaining insight about the ongoings in our souls is *the fruit in our life*.

Therefore, in this chapter we will do a deep dive into understanding this fruit, and what it can tell us. We will learn some priceless truths here, such as: why God designed us to produce certain fruit; how to connect the dots between our fruit and what is going on in our inner being; the great potential these have to lead us, protect us, bless us, and, of course, to be *re-minded*.

More specifically, we will see how our focus—particularly what we set our minds on—is directly related to the fruit in our lives, whether good or bad.

> For those who live according to the flesh *set their minds on the things of the flesh*, but those who live according to the Spirit, *the things of the Spirit*. For **to be carnally minded is *death*, but to be spiritually minded is *life and peace*.**
>
> — ROMANS 8:5-6

If God declares something to be a matter of life or death, we should be all ears. In other words, we should give our full attention to what He is saying, and do all we can *to learn and apply* what He is teaching us in that area. Why? Because, of course, so much of our life depends on it. More specifically, the consequences can be exceedingly destructive, if not deadly. Or, in contrast, they can be filled with hope, growth, and peace.

So, in His Word above, God makes plain for us this powerful cause and effect:

> *What we set our mind on can be a matter of life or death.*

In addition, there are two huge factors here: not only is God making *a profound promise* of incredible blessings, He is also giving us *a dire warning*:

- To the degree we *set our mind* our what *the Spirit desires*, we will produce *"life and peace"*

- To the degree we *set our mind* on what *our sinful nature desires*, we will produce *"death"*

To be clear, "death" does not always mean *literal* death. It often means *the absence of life*, such as the lack of an abundant life—and the lack of joy, hope, and other desired fruit (cp. Jn 10:10; Gal 5:16-23; 6:7-8; 2 Cor 3:5ff). On the other hand, "life" usually means life-giving fruit *that comes from the Giver of life*, like comfort, security, freedom, and peace of mind.

> ...and *the peace of God*, which surpasses all understanding, will *guard your hearts and minds **through Christ Jesus***.
>
> — PHILIPPIANS 4:7

> But ***the fruit of the Spirit*** is love, joy, peace, long-suffering, kindness, goodness, faithfulness, gentleness, self-control.
>
> — GALATIANS 5:22-23

The Fruit Betrays The Root

> A good man *out of **the good treasure of his heart** brings forth good*; and an evil man out of the evil treasure of his heart brings forth evil. ***For out of the abundance of the heart his mouth speaks.***
>
> — LUKE 6:45

When it comes to life or death, learning to examine, understand, and rightly respond to the fruit in our lives can literally be life-saving, as well as life-giving. The fruit we produce *outwardly* is, for the most part, a barometer of what is going on *inwardly*. In other words, our outer fruit reveals a lot about our inner being, as we learned from Martha's story. Simply put, the fruit in our lives is an invaluable *window to our souls*.

While this fruit can affirm the right treasures, beliefs, and focus of our hearts, it can also alert us to possible problems as well as highlight what needs to change in our inner being (cp. Matt 6:19-23; 15:7-9; Lk 6:45; Rom 8:5-6). This is the perfect and God-designed set up for us to be *re-minded*.

It is no wonder then that God—in His perfect wisdom and love—lovingly exhorts us to *guard our hearts* with the utmost vigor. Why? Because, just as your physical life heavily depends on your physical heart, so your overall life depends on your non-physical heart.

> *My son, **give attention to my words**;*
> *Incline your ear to my sayings.*
> ***Do not let them depart from your eyes;***
> ***Keep them in the midst of your heart;***
> *For **they are life** to those who find them,*
> *And health to all their flesh.*
> *Watch over your heart **with all diligence**,*
> ***For from it flow the springs of life.***
>
> — PROVERBS 4:21-23

Fortunately, the biblical understanding of the heart and fruit connection gives us many opportunities to be *re-minded* and make the right inner changes (e.g., Ps 51:6; cp. Jas 4:1ff; Matt 6:19-34). To the degree we take advantage of God's design and make these changes, we will know God and His love on a deeper level. This, in turn, will produce much better fruit in our lives, just as God intended.

15 VITAL BIBLICAL PRINCIPLES

With all that in mind, here are fifteen indispensable principles for us to cement in our hearts and apply to our lives. While the first few realities may be the most challenging, at least at first, they can also be the most beneficial.

1. Divinely Designed

God intentionally designed us to experience painful and unwanted feelings—and He did so out of love in order to greatly help us. These unpleasant feelings—especially stress, anxiety, and depression—are *not* malfunctions, disorders, diseases, or illnesses. But, many people erroneously believe and teach exactly that. However, just like all other undesired feelings—such as loneliness, resentment, hunger, tension, exhaustion, conviction, and physical pain—these were perfectly and *purposefully* designed by our perfect, all-knowing, loving God to function as necessary and invaluable *indicators* and *motivators*.

2. Misunderstanding God's Design Brings Harm

Much of our life and well-being hinges on the proper understanding of this divine design. Unfortunately, an untold amount of damage has been done—and continues to occur—through the wrong teaching regarding this pivotal area of life. More specifically, these erroneous beliefs are harming others—particularly by hindering them from finding the relief and solutions through the right way.

3. The Potential Blessing of Painful Feelings

Although these feelings can be exceptionally distressing, they can also be especially helpful—and even *life-saving*. How so? God intentionally designed them to serve several vital functions: they *alert us* to likely problems. They also *instruct us* and help us *connect the dots* between the fruit we are experiencing and the ongoings in our mind, heart, and life, such as: faulty thinking; focusing on the wrong things; living as if we are under the Old Covenant; putting too much hope in the wrong things; neglecting the right things; and possible dangerous people or circumstances in our life. While the right understandings here are highly beneficial, that is not enough. God also designed these feelings to *motivate us* to do something about these potentially destructive problems, *and* to make the necessary changes to resolve these harmful issues.

4. Persisting Problems

To the degree we miss out on this basic understanding of God's perfect design, we will miss out on overcoming so many common struggles in our life. This is especially true when it comes to what people struggle with the most, including things like: anxiety, stress, depression, fear, anger, insecurity, bitterness, shame, sinful behavior, damaged or harmful relationships, and addictions (i.e., destructive dependencies). What is more, if we do not rightly respond and make the necessary corrections, then these motivators will become even more pronounced, not to mention more painful. This is by design. They are intended to persist, and to increasingly motivate us to address *the root cause* of our problems. Why? Because if we do not deal with the actual cause, then our troubles will not only remain, they will likely get worse and worse. However, keep in mind that, because we live in a sinful, fallen world—which affects everything, including how well our bodies work—these indicators and motivators will not always function perfectly.

5. One Cause Of Anxiety & Depression

Let's walk through a specific example for how this works. The more we focus on what we do *not* control, the more *anxiety* we will experience. If this pattern continues, we will likely become *depressed* (e.g., hopeless). Why? Because focusing on what we do not control will, of course, produce stress and anxiousness. In addition, trying to control what we cannot control is, by definition, *hopeless*. Consequently, a prolonged pursuit of what is *impossible*—which will lead to us failing over and over, with no hope of success—will *necessarily* produce an increasing amount of hopelessness in us (e.g., depression; despair). However, this can be invaluable. How so? This fruit gives us *a window to our soul*—as these painful feelings alert us to a significant problem in our thinking and focus, and in how we are approaching at least one area of life. This not only helps us detect the cause of our stress, anxiety, and depression, it also helps with the solution (i.e., being *re-minded*). And, in very simple terms, being re-minded here is this: to shift our focus onto what we *do* control—and to lovingly and faithfully fulfill that particular part of life—while entrusting to God the outcome, and all that we do not control (cp. Jer 2:13; 17:5-8; Ps 1:1-3; 55:22; Prov 28:13; 2 Tim 1:12; 2:25).

6. Addressing The Symptom, Not the Cause

Unfortunately, the prevailing ideologies in this area are largely or solely focused on getting rid of the unwanted feeling (e.g., anxiety). While that is always *a* goal—and a very important goal—it is not *the* goal. Why? This common, yet faulty, approach is like merely turning off the irritating indicator light on our car's dashboard (e.g., "Check Engine")—rather than learning *why* it is on, and *addressing the cause* of this warning. Yet that is essentially what most people are taught to do. Therefore, they thwart the design and seek to shut off the invaluable indicator light rather than actually check the engine, and resolve the problem that caused the light to come on in the first place.

7. The Reason & Outcome

The widespread acceptance of this harmful approach is largely due to the misunderstanding or rejection of God's design, a low view of His Word, the embrace of the world's wisdom, and a *humanistic* view of humanity (e.g., that we are soulless beings). As a result, millions, if not billions, of people will spend much of their life merely trying to get rid of or cope with these distressing feelings—all without ever really understanding or addressing the actual cause of their painful and unwanted feelings. That could be the number one reason why these serious problems are getting worse and worse in our society overall, and why so many people are increasingly stressed, anxious, hopeless, and depressed.

8. There Is Always Hope

There is an abundance of good news here, namely this: the overall reality is never hopeless, especially for the believer. What is more, it is always possible for us to be *re-minded*. In other words, we can always change our understanding, our focus, and our hearts—particularly by setting our hearts on what does produce hope, and turning away from what is hopeless (e.g., Ps 42:4-5; 62:5-8; Prov 4:21-23; Lam 3:19ff; 2 Cor 4:16-18; Rom 8:5-6; 12:2; 15:4, 13; Col 3:1ff).

9. Old Covenant Living

Here is another specific example which is also very common: when it comes to the unpleasant feelings of guilt, shame, condemnation, and unworthiness, these, too, can be *a life-giving window to our soul*. How so? Because the more we experience these things, the more likely it is that we are dwelling on our past sin and failures, or past shaming from others. In the bigger picture, it often signals that we are living *as if* we are under the Old Covenant (e.g., condemnation; the law; see Gal 3:1-5; Rom 8:1ff)—and not living in the New Covenant (e.g., grace; truth; faith; God's sufficiency; cp. 2 Cor 3:5-18). Thankfully, this, too, can always be changed. Which, in turn, will produce many blessings. A simple and quick solution here is to be *re-minded* by calling to mind and resting in the reality that we are not under the law or under condemnation, but under grace, and the New Covenant (e.g., Rom 8:1-2; Gal 3-5). [There is much more that goes into this, which we go into greater detail elsewhere.]

10. The Life-Giving Response To Sin

When it comes to *godly sorrow* and *worldly sorrow*, this is also a matter of *life and death*, figuratively *and* literally (see 2 Cor 7:8-11). How so? Godly sorrow is a life-saving pain and grief, and worldly sorrow is usually a counterfeit of godly sorrow. Worse, worldly sorrow is always destructive, if not deadly (it "produces *death*"; 2 Cor 7:10). While we all sin, we will, ideally, have a certain kind of pain regarding our sin, such as: conviction; remorse; genuine contrition; and deep empathy for the pain we caused by our sin (see Ps 32; 51). Motivated by this specific kind of sorrow—which comes from love and the fear of the Lord—we then move toward God, grace, truth, repentance, and true reconciliation with God and others. Even better, this keeps us from many things, such as: beating ourselves up; wallowing in shame; fixating on the past; dwelling in regret; making excuses; destructive negative self-talk; blame-shifting; etc. Note that some of these harmful responses (e.g., heaping condemnation on ourselves) are *indicators* that we are living as if we are under the Old Covenant. On the other hand, true godly remorse—along with full confession, seeking and receiving forgiveness, living in grace, and true repentance—*indicates* we are living by the New Covenant, with life-giving godly sorrow. This, then, leads to true reconciliation, and to true peace, at least with God. Therefore, properly understanding and living according to these painful feelings will lead to life and blessings. But, if we get this wrong—especially if we live according to our sinful nature or the world's wisdom—it will lead to many destructive outcomes.

11. The Performance-Based Mindset

Similar to the above, the more we focus on *our performance*—and the more we believe we need to *earn* love, worth, or salvation through our performance, or try to find our identity in our performance—the more we will experience stress, anxiety, insecurity, fear, disappointment, condemnation, and hopelessness (e.g., depression). Why? One main reason is that this way of life is *impossible*. We will always fall short. No matter how much we do, no matter how well we do things, it will never be enough. Therefore, this will eventually produce despair and depression. However, if we rightly understand these undesirable feelings, we can then take advantage of God's blueprint. These particular unwanted feelings are *indicators* that are sounding the alarm that we are living according to a performance-based mindset. They also tell us that we are involved in a hopeless endeavor (e.g., earning love; finding sufficient value in our performance, and in what people think of us). Adding insult to injury, it is common—while living in this dynamic—to doubt our salvation as well as question God's love for us. The good news is, while this *alerts us* to an Old Covenant mode of operation, such pain and grief can also *motivate* us to correct this pain-producing problem. The particular solution here is to live more and more in the New Covenant as we: walk by faith, in grace and truth; stop striving *for* love, but instead live *from* love; and find our security, value, and sufficiency in God alone. In other words, we need to be *re-minded* that our identity and worth is found only in God, through His grace, power, love, and gospel. Sadly, it is exceedingly common for wonderful Christians to forget these truths, and to live as if they are under the Old Covenant. It will greatly bless every believer to *frequently* and *proactively* remind themselves to rest in and live in the New Covenant, and all the truths and blessings therein.

> For this reason I will not be negligent *to remind you always of these things*, though you know and are established in the present truth. Yes, I think it is right, as long as I am in this tent, *to stir you up by reminding you* ...
>
> — 2 PETER 1:12-13

12. The Fear of Man Is A Snare

A snare is "something by which one is entangled, involved in difficulties, or impeded." The more we focus on and put our hope in what people think of us—when we *need* their approval, and *fear* their disapproval—the more our lives will be impeded by anxiety, stress, and insecurity. And the more we live according to the fear of man, the more likely it will produce hopelessness and depression, among other entanglements. Again, and on the positive side of this, these distressing feelings serve a vital purpose in our lives. They provide a window to our soul—and, more specifically, they are very helpful, albeit painful, *indicators* that we are living in the fear of man. Not only that, they are designed by God as powerful *motivators* that motivate us to be *re-minded*—to change our hearts and to correct where we are placing our hope, so that we can avoid more damage and replace this bad fruit with life-giving blessings (e.g., Jer 17:5-8; Col 3:23-24). But such results can only happen if we accurately understand and respond to these unwanted feelings as God designed (i.e., they are purposeful prompts to be re-minded). On the other hand, if the universal problem of the fear of man is assessed to be a disorder or disease—or if we merely seek to cope with or get rid of these distressing feelings—then we will be plagued by them for the rest of our lives. It's worth noting that the biggest hurdle in overcoming this (and other similar problems) is giving up the disorder/malfunction/illness construct. Only then can we embrace and apply God's perfect design.

13. Motives & Perspective

The more we read and focus on God's Word with the wrong attitude or motivation (e.g., intellectualism; merely to "check the box" on a task completed; with a performance-based mindset; to be a good Christian; as a "have to," not a "get to"), the more we will miss out on the hope, joy, peace, growth, comfort, and security that comes from time in the Word. If this goes on long enough we may even start to doubt our salvation. Why? Largely because this approach will not produce the expected fruit. However, with the right understanding, this lack of desired fruit, and the presence of unpleasant fruit can actually be very beneficial. How so? While this fruit is very much undesired, it is an extremely helpful *window to our soul*—and it informs us that we are likely approaching the Word with motives or perspectives that are less than ideal, such as the ones listed above. Thankfully, all of this can change, as we daily seek to refine our motive, perspective, and purpose in reading and dwelling on His Word of life. For example: "But his *delight* is in the law of the Lord" (Ps 1:2). [See also Ps 18:30; 19:7-11; 56:10-11; 119:20, 24; Is 66:2; Mk 4:19; Lk 6:46-49; Jn 5:39-47; 1 Thess 2:13; Col 3:15-17; cp. Matt 15:3-9]

14. Bad Fruit Likely Indicates A Bad Focus

The more our mind is filled with the wrong things—and the more we focus on negative things, rather than the blessings and the truth of God's Word, with the right heart—the more we will *lack* hope, joy, peace, etc. In addition, we will also likely experience several unwanted feelings, such as stress, resentment, depression, and anxiety (Lam 3:1-20). However, all of this can actually be helpful as these painful feelings and the lack of desired fruit are very informative. More specifically, they are telling us that there is a problem. Better yet, we can take advantage of this information—exactly as God intended—to be *re-minded* by making the proper changes in our minds and hearts.

15. Good Fruit Likely Indicates A Good Focus

Conversely, the more we focus on the right things, the more hope, peace, and joy we will experience (Phil 4:8; Col 3:1-4, 15-17). Again, all this fruit—or the lack thereof—gives us *a much needed window to our souls*, as well as serving as vital *indicators* and *motivators*. What is more, much of our life and wellbeing depends on how well we understand God's divine design—and on how well we live accordingly (i.e., being *re-minded*). For more on this topic, see our article: *31 Ways To Know True & Lasting Peace*

We have one or more motivations for everything we do (e.g., being kind; doing the dishes; praying; going to work, church, school, the gym, etc.). And, as we know all too well, pain is a powerful motivator. In addition, the pursuit of desirable feelings—like peace and joy—is also a compelling motivation. However, while all of these can be helpful, our ultimate motivation should not be merely to get rid of pain and fear, or to obtain good feelings. Rather, our motives, especially when it comes to making changes in our life, should be *love*—love for God, love for others—and *trusting* in the Lord and His Word.

In other words, when something is not right within us, pain can be very useful, as it is often a necessary indicator and motivator to some degree. And, on the other hand, the motivation to attain desirable fruit (peace of mind), if understood and sought correctly, can be beneficial as well. However, our *ideal* motivation should not be feelings-focused, instead it should be God-centered, and love-centric (Matt 6:1ff; Col 3:23-24).

> Watch, stand fast in the faith, be brave, be strong. *Let all that you do be done with love.*
>
> — 1 CORINTHIANS 16:13-14

Because it is so vital to rightly understand and live according to God's blueprint, several questions will be asked to help refine and deepen your understanding here.

APPLICATION & DISCUSSION

+ How would you explain to a ten year old how our fruit is *an invaluable window to our soul*?

+ What are at least 3 to 5 things that stood out to you the most from all of the above principles?

+ Which ones are likely the hardest for people to agree with? Why is that?

+ Which ones, when applied, will have the greatest impact on you, your heart, and the fruit in your life? Why those?

+ How would you explain the *hope* and *help* that can be provided by the right understanding of unwanted feelings?

+ While God's design of unwanted feelings seems fairly obvious, why do so many people end up with a distorted view of this?

+ Why do so many Christians reject—or least not take advantage of—this seemingly straightforward understanding of this invaluable area of life?

+ How might the erroneous view lead to thwarting God's design and to harming people?

+ What would happen to us if—instead of feeling conviction, remorse, and godly sorrow—we felt lasting joy and peace when we indulged in sin, especially sin against others?

+ What would that kind of design say about God?

+ Given that same scenario (i.e., after sinning, we experienced desirous things like joy), what would happen to our relationships with others when we sin against each other?

+ What would happen to our relationship with God?

+ When it comes to spending time in God's Word, do you see this more as a way to grow *intellectually*, or do you see it as a way to grow *inwardly*, by progressively conforming your heart to His Word?

+ What might the fruit in your life indicate about this?

+ What might you need to change in your heart's attitude toward Scripture?

As we have learned, the fruit in our life is not just a matter of good fruit or bad fruit, pleasant or unpleasant. Our fruit is *a priceless window to our soul*—as God designed us with certain painful indicators to be a life-enhancing, and life-saving warning system.

There are many ways this plays out in our life, much of which we are likely unaware. Therefore, here are several common-yet-helpful examples of what our anxiety, stress, and depression are often alerting us to.

As you read the following list, think about which of these might be going on in your mind and heart.

29 Things Your Anxiety Might Be Telling You

"You're spending too much time with people who are adding stress to your life—who are not really interested in changing and growing—and are more focused on taking from you rather than having a healthy, *two-way* relationship with you."

"You are focusing too much on what you cannot control."

"You are *not* focusing on and following through with what you can and should do."

"You're comparing yourself with others."

"You're grumbling and complaining about your circumstances."

"You need to grow in gratitude, and in giving thanks to God for your many blessings."

"You have a significant struggle with being controlling—and not trusting God and His ways—and not entrusting your concerns to Him."

"You are taking on way too much responsibility" (e.g., too much on your plate; or taking too much blame for real or perceived failures in life and relationships).

"You're not taking responsibility for what you did" (e.g., making excuses; blame-shifting; minimizing; justifying; etc.).

"You have a significant problem with a *performance-based mindset*, and are trying to find your worth and identity in your performance."

"You're putting way too much hope in people."

"You care way too much about what people think of you."

"You're fretting over what others are doing, or not doing, rather than focusing on God, His love, and what you can do."

"You're putting way too much hope in _____" (e.g., job; money; appearance; performance; spouse; kids; school).

"You need to go to _____ (e.g., your friend, spouse, etc.) and work out the problems between you" (cp. Matt 5:23-24; 18:15-17; Eph 4:30-32; Col 3:12-14).

"You need to seriously consider changing the dynamics of your relationship, or lessening or severing your relationship with someone in your life."

"You're overthinking things, and not entrusting your concerns to God."

"You're living as if you are under the law, and under *condemnation*, and not under grace and truth."

"You're focused mainly on the negative things, and you're not focusing on the many wonderful things in life."

"You are picking up past offenses and re-living these painful things in your mind and heart."

"You need to truly and fully forgive _____" (e.g., Joe; Jane).

"You need to reconsider how much trust you are putting in _____" (Joe; Jane).

"You're trying to earn love—which is *impossible*—rather than, as a true believer, resting in and rejoicing over God's abundant, all-sufficient love for you."

"You're striving for love, rather than *living from love*."

"You are fixating on and obsessing over a false need" (e.g., OCD often fits here; needing others to fill your love tank/respect tank).

"You're focusing mostly on just gaining knowledge—and on an intellectual pursuit of God or theology—rather than growing in your relationship with the person of God and conforming your heart to and delighting in God's Word."

"You are feeding a destructive narrative in your mind, which is producing your _____" (fear; anger; frustration; anxiety; hopelessness; bitterness).

"You're not really spending sufficient quality time with God and His Word, or trusting Him and resting in His love, truth, and promises."

"You have significant sin in your life, which you need to address with God, and possibly others" (cp. Ps 32; Prov 28:13; 2 Cor 7:10-11).

How can we save ourselves so much needless grief and pain? By training ourselves to properly discern the unpleasant feelings in our lives—and to detect the problems that are causing them (as in the previous list)—and to respond as God intended. Being *re-minded* here will cause us to grow by leaps and bounds (Heb 5:14; 2 Cor 10:3-5; Eph 4:11ff). What is more, correcting our understanding and responses can, at least in some extreme situations, literally save a person's life, and *even their soul* (Jas 5:19-20; 2 Cor 7:8-11).

+ What, specifically, did you learn from assessing yourself in the list above?

+ How will you now take advantage of these painful feelings as God designed them to be used?

Bonus Questions

Some of the most simple yet helpful questions are never asked. These, however, can greatly benefit us, and give us great insight into our hearts, especially when needed the most. So, when you are struggling with things like stress, anxiety, or depression—or if you lack joy, peace, hope, or security—then use these as a window to your soul. With this in mind, take this time to probe your mind and heart by finishing the following sentences ...

+ The reason I lack **joy** is:

+ The reason I lack **peace** is:

+ The reason I lack **hope** is:

+ The reason I lack **security** is:

+ The reason I am **anxious** is:

+ The reason I am **depressed** is:

+ The reason I am overly **stressed** is:

+ The reason I am **fearful** is:

+ The reason I am **resentful** is:

Speaking of being resentful, it's important to understand that *resentment is a choice*. It is not something that happens *to* us. In other words, we are not bitter or resentful of others because of some painful offense against us. Rather, we experience these miserable things because we are falling short of truly and fully forgiving those who have hurt us (cp. Matt 6:14-15; 18:21-35; Eph 4:31-32).

Forgiving past offenses can certainly be challenging, especially if we do not have the right understanding and appreciation of biblical forgiveness. However, we do not have to be stuck with the ugly fruit that comes from unforgiveness. There are always solutions to this, and, therefore, there is always hope! [We have much more on this topic at **HopeForLifeOnline.com/resources**]

APPLICATION & DISCUSSION

+ After examining all your answers, what patterns can you detect in your heart, soul, and mind?

+ When it comes to finishing the previous sentences, to what degree are these reasons focused on what is *outside* of you (e.g., your circumstances and the people in your life), rather than what is *inside* of you (the things you can change like your focus, your trust in God, choosing to forgive, your time with God and His Word)?

+ What does all of that tell you, particularly about the treasures of your heart, and where you place your hope?

11

CAUTION ABOUT COUNTERFEITS

> *... lest Satan should take advantage of us;*
> **for we are not ignorant of his devices.**
>
> — 2 CORINTHIANS 2:11

Our goal as believers is to be loving, biblical, helpful, and Christlike —and to be safe from harm. However, these lofty goals come with a frequently neglected yet absolutely necessary requirement which is: *to avoid deception and error* (Gal 6:7-8; Eph 5:6; Col 2:4, 8; 2 Thess 2:3; 1 Jn 3:7). Why is this an absolute must? Because error and deceit *always* cause damage in the lives of everyone they touch—and in our society as a whole—which obviously defeats the purpose of our supreme goals (e.g., love; being like Jesus; etc.).

With that in mind, and in order to not be ignorant of the schemes of the Deceiver, we will now spend ample time addressing the dangers of *counterfeits*, particularly when it comes to the topics of meditation, focus, and renewing our minds.

A simple foundational truth to start off with is this: everything good and godly has been counterfeited. For example, there is only one true God, and one true Jesus, but there are numerous counterfeits of God, and of His one and only Son. In fact, Jesus Himself warned us about these evil imposters when He told us there would be many "false Christs" who come in His name (Matt 24:24).

In addition, there is only one way to the Father (Jn 14:6), and to be saved (Acts 4:12). However, our diabolical adversary has devised many perversions of God's good news (Gal 1:6-9).

Meditation

More specifically, and for our purposes here, there is only one true way of biblical mediation, yet there are numerous counterfeits.

What are these harmful imitations? How can we spot them? The best way to detect a counterfeit is to thoroughly know the truth, and to be intimately familiar with the real deal. What, then, is the true and right kind of meditation?

In short, biblical meditation is *filling our mind* with *God's written Word*. Not only that, we also *fully engage our mind and heart* by delighting in His truths, and resting in and believing His promises. In addition, we take time to think long and deep about how these realities apply to life, especially our personal walk with God. Better yet, this is one of the prime ways we can be proactively and reactively *re-minded*.

Very few things, if anything, will bless us more than true, biblical meditation—this includes a renewed mind and a calmed and quieted soul. What is more, these blessings are clearly spelled out in Scripture (cp. Josh 1:8-9; Ps 1:1-3; 119:27, 47, 97, 99). Therefore, in his attempts to thwart and harm us, it makes perfect sense that our evil enemy will mass produce counterfeits of this supreme blessing. Unfortunately, far too few Christians are aware of this, or can sufficiently articulate what these counterfeits are.

To help us sort this out, we will highlight one definitive night and day contrast between the right and wrong ways of meditation.

> **Biblical Meditation** is dependent upon and requires a written, *objective*, unchanging, and truly divine standard, which has been known for millennia—the Bible.
>
> **Counterfeit Meditation**, while trying hard to appear similar to the real thing, is *diametrically opposed to biblical meditation*, as it is *thoroughly subjective and feelings-based*—and involves a nebulous, mystical, and unknown spirit realm.

Therefore, even though they both use similar or identical words, it is impossible for them to be more different. In other words, while there are similarities *outwardly*, inwardly and in reality they are polar opposites and, therefore, opposed to each other.

Common Objections

A couple of common objections here go something like this: "Yeah, but ... I practice *Christian* mysticism," or, "Well, I just do exactly what other wonderful Christians do, including my pastor and well known authors," and, "Yeah, but ... I use a method that has some Scripture!"

First, there is no such thing as Christian mysticism. If there was, then we would find numerous verses and obvious examples in Scripture. But we find none.

Second, while we know there is non-Christian mysticism, trying to Christianize what is non-Christian does not make it Christian. In fact, it makes it far, *far* worse.

Third, yes, there are one or two imitations that might *start* with some Scripture (e.g., Lectio Divina), but this just adds to the deception. How so? Because it gives a false sense that the practitioner of this man-made (at best) technique of mysticism is relying on God's Word. Yet, despite how it may begin, this methodology soon turns into *an entirely subjective experience* in which the purpose is to practice this medium in order to receive subjective direction from God, a direct and subjective message from Him, or some kind of *mystical union with God Himself.* Again, there is no such technique in Scripture. However, these approaches are all found in the New Age, the Occult, and Eastern religions.

No matter how a mystical practice might start—or how it is presented outwardly—we need to look under the hood and examine the overall functional process, its goals, its source, and how it ends (Prov 14:12). And, as with everything else, we need to test all of this by Scripture (cp. Acts 17:11; Phil 1:9-11; 1 Thess 5:21; 1 Jn 4:1-6).

In so doing we will confirm that—apart from any Christian veneer—there is no real difference between so-called "Christian mysticism" and "non-Christian mysticism" (e.g., New Age). And no, this is not the conclusion of "modern day Pharisees" who are "trying to put God in a box." Rather, it is a fact openly declared by many experts in mysticism.

> Christian mysticism seems, from the beginning, to have had an intuitive recognition of the way in which mysticism is *a form of unity that transcends religious difference* ... **no absolutely clear distinction can be drawn between Christian and non-Christian mysticism.**[1]
>
> — CARL MCCOLMAN

Adding even more concern, counterfeit meditation both in function and practice—and in direct contrast to the genuine article—generally involves various ways of *emptying one's mind*. For example, the practice of repeating a word or phrase over and over (e.g., mantras; the Jesus prayer) in order to help one obtain an empty mind, and to be void of thought.

Where do we find any instance or directive to empty our minds in God's Word? The simple answer is that we do not, at all, ever. Instead, we find the exact opposite. We are called to *fill our minds with the Word of God*, as we consistently ruminate on His Word, while also thinking deeply about the practical applications of God's written Word to our hearts and lives.

> *Meditate*: The Hebrew word used for "meditate" means "muse," which means "to reflect," and *"to be absorbed in thought"*—which is, of course, the polar-opposite of *"to be void of thought."*

In stark contrast, the goal to stop thinking and to actually cease one's thought process is the heart and soul of mysticism. Again, and this cannot be emphasized enough, that approach is the antithesis of biblical meditation, not to mention of common sense. However, according to the experts in mysticism (i.e., "all mystical writers"), the elimination of our thinking is not optional. In fact, it is absolutely required.

> ***Do not reflect** on the meaning of the word; **thinking and reflecting must cease**, as all mystical writers insist.* Simply "sound" the word silently, ***letting go of all feelings and thoughts.***[2]
>
> — WILLIGIS JAGER, ZEN MASTER

While these mystical methods come with an alarming requirement (e.g., "thinking and reflecting must cease"), this actually serves as **a massive warning** to anyone using their discernment: you can *only* have success—such as peace of mind, or a direct experience with God—after you have *completely emptied your mind and stopped thinking.*

But where is that in Scripture? Does that sound like the God of the Bible? Not only is this practice in direct opposition to being absorbed in thought, and to filling and engaging our mind, it is found no where in Scripture. Not one verse. Even more alarming, this is *diametrically opposed to God's Word*. Worse yet, wittingly or unwittingly, one goal here is to circumvent and add to what God has written in His Word. And while that is not always the known objective, it is the functional end result. With all that on its resumé, how can anyone declare such a practice to be biblical, or even quasi-Christian?

Objectives

While we have touched on some goals of these mystical practices, the overall objectives are worth fleshing out even more. As we have discussed, those who practice non-biblical meditation—including many self-proclaiming Christians—are usually seeking *a supernatural word from God*, or *a direct and personal experience with God*. Not only that, this occurs in an uncertain, undefined, unknown, and unknowable spiritual realm, all of which is *wholly subjective*. Again, where is this explained and encouraged in Scripture?

In addition, this practice is also at the heart of how self-proclaiming "modern-day prophets" and new "Apostles" operate (New Apostolic Reformation (NAR) and "Word of Faith" movement). This involves those who claim to have a "fresh word from God" (as opposed to the stale Word of God? cp. Heb 4:12; Deut 32:47; Ps 1:2-3; 19:7-11; 138:2). However, in reality, this "new" information competes with and trumps God's written Word—but only in the minds and beliefs, of those who are beguiled by them.

Some may ask, "Are you saying God does not speak to us today?" No. While God has already spoken to us sufficiently and abundantly in His written Word, He can also lead and teach us in other ways. But He never, ever speaks to us through a man-made (at best) technique that is also practiced in Eastern religions, the New Age, the Occult, and by those who are wholly opposed to biblical Christianity. Nor does God ever teach or even hint that we should practice something by which we are *required* to *empty our minds* and *cease discerning*, so that *only then* can we hear God speak to us directly in a fully subjective way.

Why is all of this so important for us to know? Because counterfeits are not just erroneous, they are always deceitful and harmful. Far worse, not only are they often lethal, they are deadly in the worst ways possible (cp. Matt 7:13-27). Therefore, in his all-out war against us—and in seeking to fulfill his evil mission to deceive, destroy, and kill us—the Deceiver skillfully mimics what is right and godly (cp. Ex 7:10-13; 2 Cor 2:11; 11:3-4, 13-15). And, as a result, he will deceive and destroy multitudes of beguiled individuals (e.g., Matt 24:4-5).

With so much at stake, we should never take any of this lightly—not only for ourselves, but out of love and concern for others. Our loving knowledge, discernment, and efforts here could truly "save a soul from death."

> Brethren, if anyone among you wanders from the truth, and someone turns him back, let him know that *he who turns a sinner from the error of his way will save a soul from death* and cover a multitude of sins.
>
> — JAMES 5:19-20

When it comes to focus, meditation, and renewing our minds, always beware of, avoid, *and* openly warn others about counterfeits. This is especially true with *mystical* practices and techniques—which many Christians have tried to legitimize by attempting to Christianize them. For example, they often attach the words "prayer," "disciplines," "Christ," or "spiritual" to a given practice (i.e., contemplative prayer; breath prayers; centering prayer; spiritual formation). This deception—which is frequently promoted by popular teachers—progressively leads people away from true Christianity and into error (cp. 2 Cor 2:11; 11:13-15; 1 Tim 6:20-21).

> Many Christian leaders started searching for a new approach under the banner of "spiritual formation." This new search has led many

of them back to Catholic contemplative practices and medieval monastic disciplines.[3]

— BRIAN MCLAREN

We should not hesitate to take the fruit of the age-old wisdom of the East and "capture" it for Christ. Indeed, those of us who are in ministry should make the necessary effort to acquaint ourselves with as many of these Eastern techniques as possible. Many Christians who take their prayer life seriously have been greatly helped by Yoga, Zen, TM and similar practices.[4]

— THOMAS KEATING

All of this is absolutely vital to know because—as stress, anxiety, and depression have increased in our society—so has the practice (and praise) of counterfeit solutions. This is particularly true when it comes to the imitations of biblical meditation.

Some more specific examples of such things include:

- Mindfulness
- Contemplative Prayer
- Transcendental Meditation (TM)
- Guided Meditation or Visualization
- Practicing the "Presence" or "The Way"
- Repeating Affirmations
- Lectio Divina
- Finding Your "True Self"
- So-called Silence and Solitude
- Labyrinths
- Breath Prayers
- The "Jesus Prayer"
- Ancient Wisdom
- Holy Yoga

There are also things that are even more subtle, as they are unnamed and more generalized, like, "stop thinking for five or ten minutes, and just listen to what God is trying to say to you." In addition, one or more mystical practices are slipped into the Church by using *spiritual* sounding (literally) terms such as *spiritual* formation, *spiritual* directors, *spiritual* exercises, *spiritual* disciplines, etc.

So while these things may sound innocent, helpful, and, of course, "spiritual," that is exactly how deception works. The more a counterfeit resembles the real thing, the more likely people will fall for it and be greatly harmed (2 Cor 11:13-15; Gen 3:1-6).

That is why these mystical practices are never, at least at first, openly described by those teaching them as what they are in reality: "manmade techniques and occultic New Age practices by which you can—only after you fully empty your mind and stop *all* discernment—enter an uncertain spiritual realm where you will hopefully, if all goes right, avoid deception and the dark spirits therein—and, instead, have a direct experience, message, and mystical union with God Himself (or at least someone who you hope is God rather than some other spirit)."

While these harmful counterfeits have existed for thousands of years, they are rapidly growing in popularity and practice *inside of the Church*. They are also heavily relied upon in many, if not most, counseling and self-help settings (including things like hypnosis, along with the latest techniques), and in the increasingly popular realm of "self-care."

This mystical-meditation approach is especially true when it comes to dealing with painful and unwanted feelings, such as anxiety, stress, trauma, and depression. Making matters even worse, all these counterfeits are practiced and relied upon *rather than pursuing and depending on the one true, all-powerful God and His all-sufficient Word of life* (cp. Jer 2:13; Ps 1:1-3; Col 2:8).

The net effect of these imitations is to delude people through a *counterfeit peace*, which, in reality, is a fleeting feeling that comes from *mystical practices*. Not only that, it never really addresses the cause of our distress, and, therefore, it always leaves us needing more, just like an addiction. In other words, this, too, develops a very harmful dependency in the practitioner.

> [For a more thorough understanding on the dangers of mysticism, and mysticism in the Church, see Ray Yungen's book: ***A Time of Departing***][5]

Rationalizations

Some common rationalizations and responses to pointing out counterfeits and false teachings go something like this:

> *"All I know is that this helped me, and those I care about."*
>
> *"It works! Therefore, it must be good."*
>
> *"There are numerous saints and godly people who teach and practice these things, and they all speak so highly of it. So I am obviously going to take their word over yours."*
>
> *"It makes me feel much closer to God. How can that possibly be wrong?"*

It is very difficult, if not impossible, to argue with a person's experience. And these particular conclusions are not only completely subjective, they are, due to their very nature, extremely hard to measure and prove (e.g., "It works, therefore it must be true and of God"; "So-and-so says it's good, so it must be good.").

In addition, we know there are many things in life that *seem* to work, at least initially, but, as God warns us, they eventually lead to great harm, even "*death*" (Prov 14:12). In fact, that is exactly how a con job works ("con" is short for *confidence, confidence* man, or *confidence* scheme). A "con" builds *confidence* in the conned individual by first giving him something that seems good, or *is* good. There might be some truth, or something that *seems* true. However, the overall scheme is entirely false and harmful (e.g., Gen 3:6; Deut 13:1-5). Therefore, to the degree we lack ardent and accurate biblical discernment, we will likely fall for the con of the Deceiver.

[For more on this topic, see our booklet *Love & Discernment: Why We Need Both*]

Discernment

> *And this I pray, that your love may abound*
> *still more and more in knowledge and **all discernment**,*
> *that you may approve the things that are excellent,*
> *that you may be sincere and without offense*
> *till the day of Christ.*
>
> — PHILIPPIANS 1:9-10

> *I tell you this **so that no one may deceive you**
> **by fine-sounding arguments**.*
>
> — COLOSSIANS 2:4 [NIV]

When it comes to truth and discernment, what is our supreme standard for judging what is true and false? It should be—first and foremost—God's written Word (see Is 8:19-20; Jn 17:17; Acts 17:11; Rom 15:4). That may sound obvious, at least to some, but you might be shocked to know how many people try to argue that something is biblical *by not using the Bible*.

"Yeah, I know it's not exactly 'biblical,' but it works!"

> *"Yeah, the Bible warns about such things, but by speaking against this, you are pushing people away from God."*
>
> *"Yeah, there's no Scripture to support this, but I feel so much love and closer to God when I do it!"*

In fact, it is *very common* for self-proclaiming Christians to rely on things outside of Scripture; or, as we have seen, to use faulty rationalizations in their attempt to justify using or practicing things that are not biblical.

Some more examples of these "fine-sounding arguments":

> *"Yeah, it conflicts with Scripture, but we can just use it as a tool."*
>
> *"Yes, I see the issues with it, but I also know that this is very popular, and several Christian leaders endorse it."*
>
> *"As long as it might be helpful in any way, we will use it. We'll just try to avoid the problems with it."*

Tragically, these rationalizations are the "famous last words" before people head into serious deception. These beguiled individuals frequently mock, scoff at, and attack those who tried to warn them (cp. 1 Kgs 18:17-18; 2 Chron 36:15-16; Neh 9:26). Even worse, they spread these destructive deceits to others, causing an untold amount of deception and harm to the body of Christ.

In stark contrast to the previous examples, every Christian should always diligently determine whether or not an idea, teaching, or practice is supported by Scripture *by using Scripture* (Acts 17:11).

As you hopefully know by now, not only are these particular mystical techniques *not found in the Bible*, they come from and are found in *Eastern religions, the New Age,* and *the occult*—all of which are deeply opposed to true Christianity. How, then, can these mystical practices be declared to be biblical when they come from and are foundational to what zealously opposes the Bible and biblical Christianity? The simple answer is that they cannot.

Nevertheless, this reality has not stopped many believers from justifying and fiercely defending the use of false and anti-biblical ideas and methods. Making this worse, there are many who do so by twisting Scripture in an attempt to support their unbiblical practices.

Therefore, this is worth mentioning again: if mysticism was, in fact, biblical, then we would find it throughout the Bible. We would not have to strain to find it in God's Word. More specifically, we would find copious amounts of verses and overt examples in Scripture that obviously and clearly exhort all of us to frequently and specifically practice emptying our minds and to stop all discernment, because *only then* would we be able to enter a spiritual realm and receive a direct experience or message from God.

In other words, if mystical practices were important and biblical, then there would be numerous unambiguous and detailed instructions and examples of all of this in God's Word. Yet we find *zero* support. What does that tell us?

Instead, we are left with those who sacrifice so much of their credibility—particularly when it comes to how they handle God's Word (2 Tim 2:15)—by going to stunning lengths to take one or two verses, and pervert them (e.g., Ps 46:10; 1 Kgs 19:12). And they do all this in a desperate attempt to find some kind of Scriptural backing for a decidedly anti-Scriptural practice.

So, while these methods might offer good feelings, at first, they are absolutely misleading and dangerous. Unfortunately, more and more believers are falling for this con and, as a result, they are directing their lives and making decisions based on what might *feel* good, or *seem* right, rather than what *is* right and biblical. More importantly, and as God repeatedly warns us, this always has lethal consequences.

> *There is a way that **seems right** to a man,*
> *But **its end is the way of death**.*
>
> — PROVERBS 14:12

More Discernment

If in doubt, research *objective* and *biblical* sources (mysticism is *100% subjective*, and *devoid of any biblical support*). And, of course, above all else, do more studying of and research with God's Word. Never, ever follow someone or something simply because they are popular (cp. Matt 7:13-27), or because so-and-so says it is good and helpful. Wonderful people can be deceived, and are deceived, including pastors and other leaders.

It is up to each believer to always be a Berean (see Acts 17:11)—and to do so as an individual, as a married couple, and as a family—as well as a friend group, Bible study, life-group, and church. We can observe at least eight exceptional qualities in the biblically commended Berean—qualities we should seek to emulate.

8 Traits of Bereans

Discern | Practice ardent and accurate discernment (see also Heb 5:14; Phil 1:9-11; 1 Thess 5:21).

Avoid Error | Be passionate about avoiding error—not merely to be "right," but out of love and compassion—because error always leads to harm, and leads us and others away from God and other blessings.

Know The Truth | Seek to accurately know the truth because this is essential in order to know the true God and His love; to truly love God and love people; to avoid counterfeits, especially counterfeit love; and to avoid harming others with these falsehoods.

Love God's Word | Have a deep trust in, love for, and heavy dependence on God's written Word.

Think Biblically | Think for yourself according to Scripture—in other words, *think biblically*—and don't merely believe what others say or whatever is trendy among self-proclaimed Christ-followers.

Test Everything | Practice a healthy and biblical approach to Church leaders. Don't unquestioningly believe whatever is said by leaders (i.e., the apostle Paul). Instead, *test everything* by *thoroughly examining God's Word every day* to see whether the leader's words are true or false, according to Scripture.

Stand Out | Distinguish yourself from others—particularly in the godly traits above.

Seek God's Approval | Cultivate an overall character that is so outstanding—particularly when it comes to discernment, love, and God's Word—that, like the Bereans (who were deemed worthy to be honored in God's Word), you can be commended for being "more noble-minded."

Best of all, at least for the Bereans, these qualities did not merely keep them from being deceived—and, therefore, from deceiving and hurting others. These traits also played a great role in their *salvation*, and in knowing God and His love (see vs 12).

+ How well do the characteristics above describe you? How about your favorite authors? Or your favorite pastors or ministry leaders?

It is important to emphasize that these Bereans did not fully trust *the* preeminent leader of the Church at that time—the Apostle Paul—who would also become the most prolific writer of the Bible. Likewise, when it comes to us today, even though there are certainly trustworthy pastors, we should not *fully* trust any leader, Christian or otherwise. Rather, we see that the Bereans completely trusted in and relied on Scripture. As a result, they *searched God's Word every day* to see if what Paul said was true.

> Now these [the Bereans] *were more noble-minded* than those in Thessalonica, for they received the word with great eagerness, *examining the Scriptures daily to see whether these things were so.*
>
> — ACTS 17:11 [NASB]

Therefore, we should seek to follow the example of those who "were more noble-minded" and always measure everything by, and filter and test all that you read and hear through the written Word of God (e.g., Is 8:19-20; Rom 15:4). In fact, a good sign of a trustworthy Christian is that he or she encourages you to do the same.

If we had to pick just one verse that could explain the disconnect and division in the Church today—especially when it comes to pastors, authors, and leaders—Acts 17:11 would be a great choice. What we see at the present time is that there is one group who generally preaches and practices the principles in this verse, and another group who are weak, at best, in these areas. Unfortunately, the first group is relatively very small, and seems to be shrinking. Yet the second group is very large, and growing by the day (cp. Matt 7:13-14).

> [For more, see our book *A Tale Of Two Churches: Understanding The Division & Opposition In Today's Church*]

When it comes to discernment and counterfeit meditation, if, in addition to thoroughly relying on God's Word, you want a firsthand account, then ask a true believer who is also a former New Ager who fell prey to these deceptive imitations. Or read the many books that some of these individuals have written (and the many verses in these books). They often have great insight, largely because of how they were personally deceived and harmed by mystical practices. And they know more than most how God's Word does not support mysticism, at all, but only leads to profound deception and destruction. [For example: *The Light That Was Dark*, by Warren B. Smith; *Deceived No More*, by Doreen Virtue]

Most importantly, always remember this: *God, His Word, and His love are sufficient for us.* By filling our mind and engaging our heart with His Word of life, and delighting in God's Word—and ruminating on and rejoicing in Him and His love—we will be increasingly strengthened, comforted, and blessed. We can also process and overcome past pain, as well as *calm and quiet our soul.* Therefore, we do not need anything outside of God and Scripture for the much sought after hope, love, joy, and peace.

> *But **his delight** is in the law of the Lord,*
> *And **in His law he meditates day and night**.*
> *He shall be like a tree planted by the rivers of water,*
> *That brings forth its fruit in its season,*
> *Whose leaf also shall not wither;*
> *And **whatever he does shall prosper**.*
>
> — PSALM 1:2-3

> *You will keep him **in perfect peace, whose mind is stayed on You**, because he trusts in You.*
>
> — ISAIAH 26:3

> Now hope does not disappoint,
> *because* **the love of God has been poured out in our hearts**
> by the Holy Spirit *who was given to us.*
>
> — ROMANS 5:5

*For whatever things were written before were written for our learning, that we **through the patience and comfort of the Scriptures might have hope.***

— ROMANS 15:4

*Now **may the God of hope fill you with all joy and peace in believing**, that you may abound in hope by the power of the Holy Spirit.*

— ROMANS 15:13

APPLICATION & DISCUSSION

+ Before reading this, what were some of the counterfeit meditations you were aware of *inside* of the Church?

+ Which ones are you aware of now?

+ Christians are called to expose, "reprove," and warn others of error and counterfeits (e.g., Eph 5:11)—which counterfeit meditation has your church openly, thoroughly, and *specifically* warned you about?

+ What other counterfeits has your church exposed or warned of?

+ Which ones have you warned others about?

+ Which, if any counterfeit meditation is being encouraged, taught, or practiced in your church?

+ How would you, in at least 2 or 3 sentences, explain to another person the differences between biblical meditation and the counterfeit meditation that is in the Church?

+ How much, and in what *specific* ways, does *your* Church emphasize, teach, and encourage ardent and active biblical discernment?

+ What specific actions do they undertake to openly and actively *equip* people in discernment and *discerning all things through God's written Word* (e.g., 1 Thess 5:21-22; Acts 17:11; Phil 1:9-11; Heb 5:14)?

+ In what ways might they shy away from boldly equipping people in this vital area of life?

+ While discernment is an absolutely essential element of love (Phil 1:9-11)—and in avoiding deadly counterfeit love—*discernment is perhaps the single most neglected aspect of love today.* Do you agree or disagree with that statement? Why?

> [For more on the requirement of discernment in true love—and in detecting and escaping counterfeits—see ***Love & Discernment: Why We Need Both***]

12

A SURPASSING TRUTH
REAPING WHAT WE SOW

Do not be deceived, *God is not mocked;*
for whatever a man sows, this he will also reap.

— GALATIANS 6:7

Over the years I have observed this pattern: many will read a book like this, agree with the biblical principles therein, and start being *reminded*, while correcting their focus and renewing their mind. As a result, they start experiencing wonderful benefits. In other words, they are reaping what they have sown from their hard work of heart work.

However, at some point they begin to drift and, before they know it, they are effectively back where they started (e.g., a faulty focus; problems with anxiety, depression, etc.). Yet many of them seem perplexed as to why they are struggling again.

Fortunately, there is a rhyme and reason for this, and we will expound on that here. Doing so will not only help prevent this from happening to you, it will also equip you to make the necessary changes if or when this might occur.

We have gone to great lengths to present numerous biblical truths in this book, supported by hundreds of verses. All of these have the potential to bless us immensely, especially when it comes to being *re-minded*. Nevertheless, there is one basic truth that we must highlight here. Why? Because, in a way, this one seemingly small truth surpasses these many powerful truths. As mentioned above, and as God's Word plainly states:

> *We will reap what we sow.* (Gal 6:7-8; 2 Cor 9:6)

How is this one truth more important than all the others? Simply because all of these priceless truths can lose their applied value if we do not believe them, or consistently put them into practice (see Lk 6:46-49). In other words, and as has been said many times, there is a direct correlation between what we consistently occupy our minds with, and the fruit in our lives. No matter how hard we might try, no matter how good our intentions are, we cannot get around this basic truth.

Yes, there are often other factors involved. Yes, God certainly loves us, and His grace can make up for our many weaknesses. However, this does not do away with the reality that, generally speaking, we reap what we sow. And this principle is especially true when it comes to our focus, and how well we are *re-minded* when need be (Rom 8:5ff; Lam 3:19-26).

Let's take an example that is different than our focus. If I want to get in shape and lose weight, but I exercise once every three weeks, eat two dozen donuts a day, and only occasionally eat healthy food, then what should I expect? I should fully expect to reap what I have sown. This means I should expect to gain weight, continue to be out of shape, feel worse, and most likely get sick more often, among other things. To not expect this is to deceive myself. Hence, the first four words of the verse above: "Do not be deceived."

Does God still love me? Yes, absolutely. Does He still offer me His unlimited grace and power? Yes, absolutely. But those truths do not negate the reality of reaping what I sow. Do the undesired outcomes mean that God is punishing me? No. Does this mean He is a works-based God? No. Does this mean I should be steeped in guilt and shame, and should beat myself up? No. Does this mean God will not forgive my gluttony and laziness? No.

This is a practical matter—one of cause and effect. Therefore, in the example above, I am simply experiencing the fruit of my actions.

> *Can a man take fire to his bosom,*
> *And his clothes not be burned?*
>
> — PROVERBS 6:27

While I can make a clear connection when it comes to the physical areas of my life, this also applies to my mind, heart, and focus. For example:

Social Media | If I dwell on social media for two hours, especially right before I go to bed, then I should expect to be agitated, restless, not sleep peacefully, and perhaps struggle with many other issues as well (anxiety; feeling insecure; etc.).

Comparisons | If I frequently compare myself with others, then I should expect a lack of contentment and joy in my life. Instead, I can expect to experience a lot of insecurity, stress, feelings of worthlessness, despair, etc.

Negative Narratives | If I dwell on and feed a running narrative of negative thoughts in my mind—particularly about how unfair my life is, and the (real or perceived) injustices against me—then I should expect to struggle with anger, stress, resentment, a victim-mentality, and to eventually blow up on those around me (cp. Lk 10:38-42).

Struggles With Belief | If I have difficulty believing and rightly focusing on God, His love, and His many promises, then I should expect a struggle to maintain lasting joy, peace, hope, and security in my life.

Condemnation | If I frequently beat myself up and live in condemnation and shame—rather than grace and truth—then I should expect to experience ongoing anxiety, hopelessness, persistent feelings of unworthiness and worthlessness, and other problems as well.

Distractions | If I am distracted from my responsibilities, relationships, and other priorities—especially by focusing too much on my phone, or other similar distractions—then I should expect to miss out on certain relationships, fall short in faithfully fulfilling my responsibilities, and add many unnecessary stresses to my life.

Past Pain | If I focus on past offenses against me and if I call to mind and re-live past suffering, then I should expect to struggle mightily with resentment, anger, hopelessness, stress, fear, misery, clear thinking, etc.

The Fear Of Man | If I focus on and fret over what people think of me—and what I *think* they think of me—then I should expect to struggle with insecurity and anxiety (especially social anxiety), and to have other troubles in life, and in my relationships.

Lack of Structure | If I live an unstructured, haphazard life—and desire to faithfully fulfill my responsibilities—then I should expect a lack of peace of mind and ongoing struggles with stress, anxiety, depression, and persistent feelings of failure and guilt.

Lack of Time With God & In The Word | If I regularly miss spending quality time with God and His Word, then I cannot expect to have a growing personal relationship with God, and the strength, security, and blessings that come from this.

Performance-Based Mindset | If I focus on finding my identity and value through my performance—and not in God and His love and grace—then I can expect to struggle with anxiety, fear, hopelessness, stress, fear of man, persistent feelings of never doing enough, etc.

Being A Rule-Follower | If I focus mainly on *following the rules*—and not on loving and living for the Person who gave us these rules, truths, principles, and grace—then I should expect to experience a lot of stress and anxiety, regular feelings of falling short or never doing enough, as well as a lack of joy, peace, etc.

There Is Hope

Don't despair. There is hope. All of these things can change. You do not have to be a great person—or an extra-special Christian—or just work more in order to see a transformation in your life. You can grow and reap different fruit simply by remembering the we-reap-what-we-sow principle, and applying the appropriate principles in your life (i.e., being *re-minded*).

APPLICATION & DISCUSSION

+ Which areas from the list above apply to you the most?

+ In what ways might this explain any struggles in your life, *and* help you change and overcome these?

+ How would you explain the principle of we-reap-what-we-sow to another person, especially when it comes to our focus and our need to be *re-minded*?

Overall, to the degree our focus is on the wrong things—and not on what is right, true, loving, and lovely (e.g., Phil 4:8; Ps 1:1-3; Col 3:15-17)—then we should *not* expect to reap joy, contentment, peace of mind, freedom, and security. To put it another way, the truths of God's Word and principles in this book—which come from His Word—lose their meaning and impact *if we do not believe them* (1 Thess 2:13), or *if we do not put them into practice* (Matt 7:13-27).

Fortunately, this truth cuts both ways. On one hand, such a stark reality might represent a stern, and likely painful, warning. However, if we see it in the right way, *this can give us an abundance of hope.* How so? Because it not only helps us accurately diagnose why we might be struggling, it also gives us clear and very doable solutions so that we can resolve these problems (e.g., by correcting our focus and where we put our hope).

So, always remember that you reap what you sow—but never forget God's grace, love, mercy, and power. When it comes to renewing your mind and changing your heart, if you give a little, then you should expect very little. If you give half-heartedly—or if you make big changes, but revert back to your old ways—then you should absolutely expect to receive poor results. Nevertheless, this can always be changed, and you can start reaping the much desired fruit of peace, joy, and security.

If you start to experience one or more of your previously unwanted experiences—such as anxiety, depression, stress, a troubled mind, panic attacks, etc.—then ask yourself the following questions. If you are struggling in these ways, it is highly likely that you will find the necessary solutions in your answers to the questions below.

+ In what specific areas, and to what degree have I drifted from the right focus?

+ In what ways have I been focusing *too much on certain things* (e.g., phone; the news; job; sports; what others think of me; the past; my performance)?

+ To what degree and in what ways have I been focusing on *what is negative and harmful* (e.g., comparing myself; the negative things in life; injustices; social media)?

+ Did you initially make great changes to structuring your day differently (in the morning and evening), but then drifted from what you established? If so, in what ways (e.g., focusing on your phone; going to bed later, and not getting up on time; not following through on your commitments)?

13

NIGHT & DAY
PRACTICAL CHANGES

But his delight *is in the law of the Lord,*
And in His law he meditates **day and night.**

— PSALM 1:2

I recently heard a man give a spontaneous, yet brief, testimony about how a seemingly small change resulted in huge blessings in his life. For decades, his daily routine was to pick up the newspaper every morning and spend the next hour or so reading the news. However, at some point, he realized he needed a change. As a result, he decided to stop getting the paper and, instead, he started reading his Bible the very first thing in the morning. He then went on to share how that one simple change transformed so much of his life.

His encouraging story highlights two tremendous opportunities for all of us: within each day there are two pivotal times for us to focus on —the morning and evening—as these hold huge potential for a great impact in our lives, for good, or not-so-good.

More specifically, how we spend our morning, and what occupies our mind after we wake up, heavily influences us throughout our day. In addition, what we do, and what occupies our heart before we go to bed, heavily influences our sleep, and our overall peace of mind. This, then, greatly impacts us for the next day. And so on ...

With all that in mind, let's answer two simple yet vital questions.

+ How do you spend the first hour or so after you get up?

+ How do you spend the last hour or so before you go to bed?

Things that could be included here are: eating breakfast, getting ready for bed, getting dressed or undressed, etc. While those are universal activities, we are looking for more specifics, such as: in what ways, and how much time do you dedicate to spending with God and His Word, resting your mind, unwinding, prayer, etc.? These are the things we want to focus on in this chapter, and for you to pay attention to during those times of the day and evening.

Over the years I have talked with many individuals who are shocked, pleasantly so, by how much their lives improved by altering just these two things: *the beginning and end of their day*—and doing so in the right way. Believe it or not, this is equally possible for you as well.

Changing the first and last part of the day is very helpful in other areas as well, such as work, school, and relationships. This, then, can produce even more good things in our lives. For more encouragement on this, take the following wise words to heart from J.C. Ryle, a nineteenth century pastor and author:

> Read the Bible daily. Make it part of your everyday business to read and meditate on some portion of God's Word. Gather your manna fresh every morning. Choose your own seasons and hours. Do not scramble over and hurry your reading. Give your Bible the best, and

not the worst, part of your time. But whatever plan you pursue, let it be a rule of your life to visit the throne of grace and the Bible every day.[1]

— J.C. RYLE

Notice that pastor Ryle did not emphasize obtaining intellectual knowledge or being a good Christian. Nor did he merely tell us to read the Bible. While he does rightly highlight and prioritize the Word—and *meditating* on God's Word of life—he also gives the bigger and necessary context of *our relationship with God*. Even better, he encourages us to approach God through grace—and His throne of grace—and not our goodness (kind of like Mary, as opposed to her sister Martha).

APPLICATION & DISCUSSION

+ If giving God's Word "the best" of your time is a 10, and "the worst" is a 0, how would you rate yourself in how you value time in the Word on a daily basis?

+ In what ways can you connect the dots between the fruit in your life —good, bad, or in between—to the quality of your time with God and His Word?

+ In order to improve here, what tangible changes, including heart changes, can you make?

> And **let the peace of God rule in your hearts**, to which also you were called in one body; and be thankful. **Let the word of Christ dwell in you richly** in all wisdom, teaching and admonishing one another in psalms and hymns and spiritual songs, singing with grace in your hearts to the Lord.
>
> — COLOSSIANS 3:15-16

To be clear, reading the Bible is not some kind of magical cure. A person can read God's Word for an hour or two and not get much, if anything out of it. Why? Because our minds and hearts need to be actively engaged with God, through His Word of life, as we refine our focus—and as we seek to grow in our belief in His truths and in our trust in Him (Rom 15:13; 1 Thess 2:13). Therefore, these are daily opportunities to be *re-minded*, both proactively and reactively.

In addition, we will ideally "let the word of Christ *dwell in (us) richly*," and purposefully apply His Word to our lives and our hearts. Without this, we will tend to be weak and ineffective, as time in God's Word is vital for how well we function each day. All of this confirmed and expounded on by the great George Muller.

> As the outward man is not fit for work for any length of time unless he eats, so is with the inner man. What is the food for the inner man? Not prayer, but the Word of God—not the simple reading of the Word of God, so that it only passes through our minds, just as water runs through a pipe. No, we must consider what we read, ponder over it, and apply it to our hearts.[2]
>
> — GEORGE MULLER

Therefore, above and through all this we see that *there is an undeniable connection between spending quality time with God and His Word, and reaping good fruit in our life.* The opposite is also true: there is an undeniable connection between a lack in time with God and the

Word, and the lack of desirable fruit in our life. Jesus pointed out this reality when He quoted the Old Testament to Satan:

> But [Jesus] answered and said, "It is written, 'Man shall not live by bread alone, *but by every word that proceeds from the mouth of God.*'"
>
> — MATTHEW 4:4

The Put Off/Put On Principle

> ... that you *put off*, concerning your former conduct, the old man which grows corrupt according to the deceitful lusts, ***and be renewed in the spirit of your mind***, and that you *put on* the new man which was created *according to God, in true righteousness and holiness*.
>
> — EPHESIANS 4:22-24

While passion for personal growth—especially in our relationship with God—is a wonderful and necessary component for godly growth, it is not enough. In addition to this desire, we must learn and apply one of the most transformative truths God teaches us in His Word: *The put-off/put-on principle* (e.g., Eph 4:22-5:2; Col 3:5-16).

The first step here is, of course, the "put *off*." God—because He loves us so much, and wants to tremendously bless us—directs us to *"put off"* that which is erroneous, sinful, and harmful in our life.

Secondly, in its place we are to *"put on"* what is true, loving, and beneficial. One simple example would be to put off lying and to put on telling the truth instead. Another example would be to put off a bad relationship, and to put on a good relationship in its place.

Notice, however, from the Scripture in Ephesians above, that our aim is not just to improve our behavior. Nor are we to merely stop something bad and replace it with something good. The primary goal should be, as always, that *our inner being is "renewed"* (e.g., *re-minded*).

We do this by making our hearts less like our *old selves* and more like God "in true righteousness and holiness" (see also Gal 4:19; Rom 12:2).

Therefore, when we look at this in the right way, we will see many things in life that we *get to* put off, and *get to* put on. For example, God instructs us to put off bitterness, rage, and malice—which are always ugly and hurtful—and, in their place, put on kindness, compassion, forgiveness, and freedom, which are always beautiful. Not only that, these things are a blessing to everyone (e.g., Eph 4:31-32).

Again, this comes about through being *re-minded*—as we renew our mind and transform our inner being, and as we rest in and rely on God and His ways (e.g., living in grace and truth). If not—if we merely change our behavior without changing our beliefs and treasures of our hearts, and without trusting God more and more—we will almost assuredly revert back to our old ways, and likely become discouraged in our growth process (cp. Mk 7:6-7).

So, in general, when we apply this put off/put on principle to our lives, not only do we *get to* get rid of what harms others, ourselves, and grieves the Lord, we—through changed hearts—*get to* replace these with what blesses others, ourselves, and God. What could be better than that? Well, actually ... through this process, we will also grow stronger, more secure, and our hearts will become more and more like Jesus (cp. Gal 4:16; Eph 5:1-2).

The overall process here, discussed in an earlier chapter, is often referred to as "sanctification," which also involves personal repentance. Repentance, from the Greek word *"metanoia,"* means: *"a change of mind."* Therefore, to the degree we improve our inner-being (e.g., renew our mind), our outer fruit will improve as well—as will our relationships (e.g., Mk 4:20).

While every human would love to simply *put off* anxiety, depression, fear, and insecurity—*and* put on love, joy, peace, and security in their place—it does not quite work that way. We cannot just put off certain undesired fruit, and then put on the desired fruit.

As we have learned: *to change the fruit, we must change the root*. This, of course, involves our hearts and focus, which includes the *hard work* of *heart work* (Prov 4:23; Phil 4:6-8; Rom 8:5-6; 12:2; Lk 6:45).

So, when it comes to this process of changing these roots—particularly by changing our focus and hearts—here are some specific aspects for us to *put off* in the morning and evening.

Things To Put Off

For the first and last hour or so of the day, here are some things to refrain from:

- Using your phone
- Doing work
- Homework
- Social media
- Checking your email
- Dwelling on financial concerns
- Dwelling on problems and drama in relationships
- Reading or watching the news
- Focusing on other areas of life that tend to be negative, and produce stress and anxiety (e.g., electronic games; reading or watching stress inducing things, including certain books, articles, movies, shows, etc.)

All of the above are your specific "put offs."

The next step is to "*put on*" the right things. This means you need to add to your life the things that will encourage you, point you to God, give you hope, lighten your load, and bless God, you, and others (e.g., 1 Pet 5:7; Matt 11:28-30; Is 26:3; Rom 15:4, 13).

Next is a list of fifteen wonderful things you *get to* put on—and to engage your heart in—so that you can daily be *re-minded* and *"renewed in the spirit of your mind,"* enabling you to overcome many challenges in your life.

15 Things To Put On

1. God's Word | *Delighting* in, *meditating* on, and *believing* God's Word of life (Ps 1:1-3; 1 Thess 2:13; Col 3:16)

2. The New Covenant | Dwelling on and delighting in the reality of *who you are in Christ*—all through *His New Covenant*—while continually distancing yourself from the Old Covenant (e.g., living under the law and under condemnation; Rom 8:1ff; 2 Cor 3:5ff)

3. God's Love | *Abiding in God and His love,* and remembering to do everything *out of love,* all *for God and His glory* (Jn 15:1ff; 1 Jn 4:16; Eph 3:16-21; Col 3:24-25)

4. Prayer | Spending time in prayer (Ps 5-7; Matt 6:9-13; Phil 4:6-7; Col 4:2; Rom 12:12)

5. Thanksgiving | Genuinely giving thanks to God (Ps 35:18; Col 1:12; 2:7; 3:15-17)

6. Promises | Reminding yourself of and resting in your favorite promises and principles of God's Word

7. Truth | Memorizing Scripture, as a get to, not a have to, and as a way to store up God's Word in your heart and mind (Deut 6:6; Ps 119:11; Prov 7:3)

8. Application | Prayerfully applying key parts of God's Word to your heart

9. Worship | Enjoying worship music, and, therefore, genuinely *worshiping God* (Ps 95:6; 100)

10. Rejoicing | Rejoicing *in the Lord,* not so much *about* your circumstances (Phil 4:4; Hab 3:17-19; 2 Cor 6:10)

11. **Eternity** | Shifting your thoughts and focus from what is temporary to what is *eternal* (Matt 6:19-21; 2 Cor 4:16-5:10; Heb 11; Ps 73:15-26; Col 3:1-4)

12. **Responsibility** | Shifting your focus away from what you cannot control, and on to what you do control (e.g., Prov 21:31; Matt 6:19-34; 2 Cor 12:9-10)

13. **Reconciliation** | Reconciling with God, which always brings peace in our hearts. If you have any unaddressed sin, then you can contritely confess this sin to God—ask Him for forgiveness, and receive and rejoice in His full forgiveness—and commit to repenting in that area (Prov 28:13; 1 Jn 1:9; Heb 4:16; cp. Lk 7:36-50)

14. **Forgiveness** | Forgiving others: if there is anyone and anything you have yet to forgive—if one or more past offenses are still hurting and hindering you—then forgive these in the right and biblical way (Eph 4:31-32; Col 3:12-14; cp. Heb 12:15; Mk 11:25; Matt 6:14-15; 18:22-35) [We have additional books to help thoroughly understand and live in forgiveness]

15. **Trust** | Unloading your burdens and *entrusting* your concerns to God, because you know He loves you, and because you trust His ways over your ways (Matt 11:28-30; Ps 37:3-8; 55:22; Is 55:8-9; Phil 4:6-7; 2 Tim 1:12; 1 Pet 5:7)

Again, this is not a list of *"have to's."* These are all *"get to's."* Also, you do not have to do *all* of these *every* day. They are simply *opportunities* for you. They are meant to be things you enjoy—which, in turn, will bless you, strengthen you, lighten your load, and give you growing security and hope.

What is more, these will also bless God, as you grow in your relationship with Him and increase your understanding of His love, truth and grace. And all of this will overflow into blessing others as well. This, in turn, will greatly benefit your relationships, and strengthen you at work, school, church, and home.

In addition, and as discussed more than once, remember that this is not merely a list of techniques to get our mind off of other things. Rather, they are all vital aspects of a relationship with God, intended for lasting joy and peace in our lives overall. These also involve our hearts, and how we live our lives *with* God, and *for* God—as well as *with* and *for* others (Phil 2:3ff; 2 Cor 5:15; Mk 12:30-31).

In other words, this is all a win, win, win, win, win. And there is no real downside.

> *It is good to* give thanks to the Lord,
> *And to* sing praises to Your name, *O Most High;*
> **To declare Your lovingkindness in the morning,**
> **And Your faithfulness every night ...**
>
> — PSALM 92:1-2

APPLICATION & DISCUSSION

+ When it comes to your focus, what, specifically, are the biggest things for you to *put off* in the morning and evening (your phone; reading the news; work; emails; texts; TV/movies; the wrong kind of music; thinking about various problems and how to solve them)?

+ What things will be the hardest for you to put off (phone; checking emails; the news; work related matters)?

+ *Why* will these be the most difficult to put off?

+ Which of the above *put on's* do you think will bless and strengthen you the most? Why those specific ones?

+ If these changes will produce so many good things, then what are the main reasons why people, in general, do not make long term changes in how they spend their mornings and evenings?

+ Which of these might apply to you?

To be clear, we are not limited to making changes *only* in the morning and evening. We can alter what we focus on throughout the day, including during lunch time and other breaks in our day. Yet, do your best to refrain from doing this as a "have to" rather than a "get to."

Making Concrete Changes

+ With the goal in mind of making tangible changes in your daily routine, think about where, exactly, you can sit in order to set aside this time with God and His Word. For example, a specific chair, at a certain table, etc. Also, in what specific ways can you better structure your time in the morning and evening [e.g., shutting down electronics at a certain time; going to bed and getting up earlier]?

As you likely know, restructuring your day can be very challenging, especially at first. Another hindrance here is that some individuals see this as legalistic or restrictive. However, no matter how we view this, if it is not done well, then we will struggle in following through on our commitments and in making lasting changes.

Therefore, be patient. Be prepared. Know that there will be obstacles—and inevitable ups and downs. There will also be a common pattern of three steps forward, and one or two steps back. You should fully expect this to happen. Prepare yourself mentally and spiritually for it, and don't be discouraged when these things occur. Keep going.

> *Bless the Lord, O my soul,*
> *And forget not all His benefits.*
>
> — PSALM 103:2

Write It Down

Brainstorm and write a list of some specific things to be grateful for, to ruminate on, and for which to give thanks to God, including:

WHO GOD IS—*The many attributes of God*

WHAT GOD HAS DONE—*The many things God has done for you*, generally and specifically (e.g., He died for you; He gave you life; and, if applicable, He blessed you with certain things, like family, friends, job, school, etc.)

WHAT GOD IS DOING—*The many things God is doing for you now* (e.g., loving you daily; helping you to change your heart in order to change the fruit in your life; listening to and answering your prayers)

WHAT GOD WILL DO—*The many things God will do for you in the future* (particularly in eternity)

Yes, doing this will take time, but it can also be very enjoyable. Continue to add to these lists—and frequently remind yourself of these things—as you give thanks to God for Who He is and all that He has done, is doing, and will do in your life.

> *... always giving thanks to God the Father for everything, in the name of our Lord Jesus Christ.*
>
> — EPHESIANS 5:20

More Good News

I have talked with many stressed and depressed individuals who were able to change their day and incorporate the above put offs and put ons. As a result, they increasingly replaced their anxiety and hopelessness with security, joy, and peace. Some of this can occur relatively right away, but long term change will not, of course, happen over night. Overall, these individuals put these things into practice over a period of time—with a fair amount of ups and downs. This is to be expected with all growth.

On the other side of this, many resist making these much-needed changes, while others make only half-hearted attempts. As a result, they continue to struggle with painful, unwanted fruit in their life. Therefore, it's important to intentionally pray about and commit to following through on the changes you want to make, and remember the *we reap what we sow* principle.

14

WHAT IS "THIS" FOR YOU?

> *Yet **this** I* call to mind *and* **therefore I have hope** ...
>
> — LAMENTATIONS 3:21 [NIV]

We have established that there is a powerful connection between calling "*this*" to our minds and going from hopeless to hopeful. Therefore, "this" needs more of our attention, as it has unlimited potential to be life-changing, and even life-saving.

The pivotal question for you here is: what is "this" that you rely on to be *re-minded*—particularly when you are distressed? In other words, when you are struggling with unwanted thoughts and feelings, what are you fully prepared to "call to mind," just like Jeremiah did in the above verse?

Whether you realize it or not, your level of preparedness here is the primary solution to many problems in life. On the other hand, a lack of being equipped in this area will cause you to be very ineffective when it comes to being *re-minded* and overcoming struggles (2 Tim 3:15-17; 2 Pet 1:3-4; Heb 13:20-21).

> Therefore, **prepare your minds for action**; be self-controlled; set your hope fully on the grace to be given you when Jesus Christ is revealed.
>
> — 1 PETER 1:13 [NIV]

Therefore, it is both wise and necessary to have an ample supply of specific Scriptures and truths ready to call to mind. This is particularly pertinent in your fight against faulty thinking, unwanted thoughts, and troubles with anxiety, guilt, depression, fear, stress, etc. For this and other reasons, we will address several vital areas in this chapter.

Always remember that we are not merely calling to mind certain truths. We are, more specifically, seeking encouragement, hope, comfort, and strength from a *Person*. And not just any person—He is *the Person* who is *the* truth, *the* way, and *the* life—and who is also the God of hope, and the One who loves us the most, by far (Rom 5:5, 8; 8:32; 15:13; Eph 3:16-21; 1 Pet 5:6-7).

This is precisely what David did, and it is one of the reasons he was considered to be *a man after God's own heart* (1 Sam 13:14):

> Now *David was greatly distressed*, for the people spoke of stoning him, because the soul of all the people was grieved, every man for his sons and his daughters. **But David strengthened himself in the Lord his God.**
>
> — 1 SAMUEL 30:6

When it comes to things like stress, anxiety, condemnation, and depression, ideally we will have prepared *ahead of time* several truths to call to mind, dwell on, and apply. By being *re-minded* in this way, we will be, like David, strengthened and refreshed by God Himself, and His grace, truth, and love.

To be clear, this preparedness should not merely be a collection of verses that we know, and then use in the heat of the moment. There must be an ever-growing *belief* in our hearts and increasing trust in these biblical truths and how they speak to and help us overcome specific struggles (e.g., Phil 4:6-8; 1 Pet 5:7). Doing this will change everything.

In what follows, we will list several common struggles *and* the corresponding verses to learn, know, believe, and apply. This will also include several biblical examples of people in similar situations (e.g., Joseph; Paul). Your goal here is not just to know these verses, it is to *increasingly believe* these truths proactively, and to consistently *rely on and call them to mind* when necessary.

Biblical Hope For Common Struggles

- *Suffering*

When you are going through suffering—trials, troubles, and tribulations—you can *call to mind* certain people, including **Job** (Job 1-42), **Joseph** (Gen 37-50), **David** (2 Sam 12:15-23), **Paul**, especially his *thorn in the flesh* (2 Cor 12:7-10), and **Jesus** (Heb 12:1-3; 1 Pet 2:21-23).

You can call to mind numerous other vital verses as well, including: Ps 94:19; Jn 15:1-2; Rom 5:3-5; 8:17-18, 28-32, 35-39; 2 Cor 1:3-10; 4:7-12, 16-18; 6:3-10; 11:23-28; Phil 1:12-14, 20-21, 29; 3:10-11; 4:11-13, 19; Heb 11:24-27; 12:5-13; 13:5-6; Jas 1:2-4; 1 Pet 1:6-9; 4:1-2, 12-14, 19.

- *Anxiety & Depression*

When stressed, anxious, or feeling depressed, *call to mind* **Jeremiah** in Lamentations 3:19-25—and how he changed the focus of his heart, which, as a result, radically changed the fruit in his life (see also Ps 23; 37; 42; 43; 73; 94:19; 131; Is 26:3; Rom 15:4, 13; Phil 4:4-8; 1 Pet 5:7).

There is obviously so much more we can learn and apply when it comes to anxiety and depression. In addition, overcoming these involves the hard work of heart work, as expounded on earlier.

We address these problems and solutions much more thoroughly elsewhere, including a book dedicated to overcoming depression, anxiety, and condemnation—and another book devoted to understanding stress and how to remove it from our lives.

- *Understanding Injustice*

When you are struggling with the injustice in the world, and a proper perspective is needed on how to understand injustices, unfairness, and suffering—especially when those who do what is right are suffering, and those who do wrong seem to go unscathed—*call to mind* **Joseph**, and his *"50/20 vision,"* based on Genesis 50:20.

You can also dwell on similar verses, people, and responses, like **Jesus** (Lk 23:34; 1 Pet 2:21-13; Heb 12:1-3), **Stephen** (Acts 7:60), Peter (1 Pet 1:6-9), and **Asaph** in Psalm 73.

See also: Ps 37; 119:67, 71, 75; 2 Cor 1:8-9; 4:16-18; Heb 12:5-13

- *Persecution For Your Faith*

When you are disdained, attacked, or persecuted for your *biblical* beliefs, *call to mind* those in Scripture who also went through such things (e.g., **Daniel; Moses; Paul; Jesus**). We can also be encouraged by how they persevered and faithfully fulfilled what God called them to do—and how they ultimately entrusted themselves and the outcome of everything to God (Dan 3; Phil 1:21; 2 Tim 1:12; 3:12-13; Heb 10:32-39; 11:1ff; 12:1-4; 1 Pet 2:20-24; 1 Sam 30:6).

What is more, while acknowledging and grieving the pain, we can also rejoice when we are persecuted. How so? Because we are living for what is right and true, and for the true Jesus, and we are blessing Him. On top of that, God promises us that He will richly reward us in eternity for boldly living for Him and His Word (Mt 5:10-12; Mk 4:17; Lk 6:22-23; 2 Cor 4:16-18; 6:10).

[To be abundantly clear, if people confront you on actual sin or error in your life, you are *not* being persecuted. If they do this, at least reasonably well, then they are doing what is right and loving, and you are not being persecuted.]

- *Anger & Resentment*

When you are hurt by others, and perhaps struggling with bitterness, anger, or resentment—and, therefore, forgiveness is needed— *call to mind* people like **Stephen** (Acts 7:60), **Jesus** (Lk 23:34), and **Joseph** (Gen 5:20), and many other verses as well (Mk 11:25; Lk 17:3; Eph 4:31-32). In addition, contrast this with Matthew 6:14-15; 18:23-35.

Also consider the woman in Luke 7:36-50 and her heart after being forgiven by God. Always make sure you are truly applying biblical forgiveness, as it is fairly common for Christians to misunderstand and misapply forgiveness.

[For more, see: ***Forgiveness, A Practical & Biblical Handbook On How To Forgive***. And also make sure you know that forgiving others does not mean you have to trust them, as detailed in another book: ***Forgiveness & Trust***]

- *Temptation*

When you are tempted with one or more sins, especially if they are reoccurring sins, *call to mind* Romans 8:5-6. This directs you to stop setting your mind on what your flesh desires and, instead, to necessarily set your mind on what God desires (see also Gal 5:16-25).

In addition to calling out to God for help and relying on His power (1 Cor 10:13; 2 Cor 10:3-5) in your battle to overcome sin, it is necessary to proactively store up His Word in your heart (Ps 119:9-11; Prov 7:3; Deut 6:6-8; Lk 6:45-49). However, never do these things in a legalistic or intellectual way. Instead, do this by truly delighting in, believing, and applying God's Word, and knowing that He gave us these truths to protect us, direct us, and bless us—and not to restrict us or keep us from happiness (cp. Deut 30:15-20; 32:47; Ps 18:30; 19:7-11; see also Eph 4:11-32; Col 3:1-16).

Temptation will often plague us if we have not truly repented of certain sins. Therefore, in order to truly overcome sin in our life, a thorough heart change is needed, particularly through *godly sorrow* and *repentance* (2 Cor 7:8-11; Lk 3:8ff; Acts 3:26; 26:17-20).

- *Why God Allows Suffering*

When you struggle to understand *why* God allows difficulties and suffering, *call to mind* **Paul's** thorn in the flesh (2 Cor 12:7-10); **Joseph's** experiences in Gen 37-50 (particularly Gen. 50:20); and **Job**, especially all the "behind the scenes" activity between God and Satan. See Psalm 37, and many other Psalms as well.

In addition, one of the most important sections of Scripture that helps us understand, if not appreciate, suffering is found in Hebrews 12:5-13 (see especially verse 5-6, and 10-11).

Also proactively study: 2 Cor 1:8-9; 4:16-18; Rom 5:3-5; 8:28-29; Jas 1:2-4; 1 Pet 1:6-9; Jn 15:1ff. In these, we see that we do not suffer just to suffer. There is incredible potential for God to do powerful things in us, and to produce wonderful things through our suffering. Yet, what is of utmost importance in suffering is that we trust God and His ways, and that we actively engage Him and His agenda in all of this (see especially the last eight words of Heb 12:11).

- *Unanswered Prayer*

When God is not answering your prayers, at least seemingly, then *call to mind* **Paul** and his thorn in the flesh (again)—and how God responded to Paul's pleadings and prayers—along with Paul's new perspective and response (2 Cor 12:7-10).

See: Is 55:8-9; 2 Cor 4:16-18; 5:7; 1 Sam 3:18; 2 Sam 15:25-26; Hab 3:17-19

- *Guilt & Shame*

When struggling with condemnation, shame, and guilt, *call to mind* the woman who was "forgiven much" (Lk 7:36-50), and other key verses as well (Rom 5:20). Another reality to *call to mind* is that we can always approach God with confidence—even when we sin and fail. Why? Because God sits on "the throne of grace" (Heb 4:16), and not a throne of shame, performance, or condemnation. He wants us to come directly to Him whenever we sin, and not stay away from Him.

Also, frequently *call to mind* the *New Covenant*, and how you, as a true believer in Jesus, are no longer under the law or condemnation, but under grace and freedom (Rom 5:20; 8:1ff; Gal 3:1ff; Gal 5:1ff; 2 Cor 3:5ff; Heb 4:16; Lam 3:22-24). This reality is a huge factor in life—which is why we have *much* more on this topic elsewhere.

- *Perfectionism*

When feeling pressure to be perfect—or if you place unreasonably high expectations of yourself (or others)—then, again, *call to mind* the *New Covenant,* and the fact that there is no need to be perfect, at all. More specifically, you can *call to mind* that you are under grace—and not the law, not condemnation, and not the need to perform in order to be accepted, loved, and worthy. Again, the New Covenant is the key. So learn the many truths and blessings therein, and increasingly live in the New Covenant (where we are sufficiently loved and valued in Christ and His grace), both proactively and reactively (i.e., before and after you sin and fail).

See: Rom 6:14; 7:4-6; 10:4; 2 Cor 3:5ff; Gal 3:1ff; 5:1ff.; Jn 1:14, 17

- *Dismayed by This World*

When you see the things in this world as increasingly bleak, hopeless, unfair, evil, and disturbing, *call to mind* **Jesus**, and how He overcame the world, and the fact that He did so for us (e.g., Jn 14:26-28; 16:33; Heb 12:1-4; 1 Jn 5:3-5). Not only that, He is the God of hope, and His Word gives us unlimited hope (Rom 15:4, 13).

Also call to mind **Asaph**. He was greatly distressed over the wickedness and many injustices in the world. However, in the midst of his dismay, he approached God with his grief and concerns, enabling him to eventually come to a place of harmony with God and His ways (Ps 73, particularly verses 15-27). For more, get to know and call to mind Psalm 23; 37; 62; Prov 21:31; Jn 16:33; Phil 1:21; 3:12-14, 18-20; Heb 11; 12:1-15; 2 Cor 4:16-5:21; Col 3:1ff; Jude 1:16-25.

Remember that your "citizenship is in heaven," and that your work in the Lord "is not in vain." Your love and faithfulness always has value to God, and you will be richly rewarded as well (1 Cor 3:12-15; 15:58; 2 Cor 4:16-18; Col 3:24-25).

- *Troubled In Mind*

When you are *over-burdened, stressed out,* and *troubled in your mind*—and perhaps struggling with intense anger, and even anger toward God—then *call to mind* **Martha**, especially in contrast to her sister **Mary** (Lk 10:38-42). Or *call to mind* **David**, and how he processed the issues in his life with God, and through this was able to *still and quiet his soul* (Ps 131). On top of all that, *call to mind* and believe and rest in other verses connected to *peace of mind* (Ps 119:165; Is 26:3; Rom 8:6; Col 3:15)—particularly Philippians 4:4-13, especially 6-7.

Also, prayerfully consider the following possibilities, which will help you get to the actual cause of what is troubling your mind: the ways in which you have taken on too much responsibility; how you might be approaching God, the Bible, and Christianity more as a duty or *intellectual pursuit*, rather than a loving relationship with the person of God; how you might be "distracted" and "drawn away" from what is most important (time with God and in His Word; resting in His love, grace, and truth); how you might be feeding a false narrative in your mind (e.g., "That's not fair." "Why do I have to ____?!" "Doesn't anyone care?" "No matter how much I do, it's not enough." "Doesn't God care about my situation?" "I'm a horrible person"); and how you might be living according to a performance-based mindset (e.g., striving to earn acceptance and find your value through your performance, and what others think of your performance).

Overall, think about how you can seek the appropriate amount of responsibility in your life (not too much, or too little)—and specifically dedicate more time to resting, and to spending quality time with God, in His Word. It may also be very beneficial to go back and re-read the material in this book on **Martha** and **Mary**.

• *Longing For A More Personal Relationship With God*

When you want to enjoy God on a more personal level, *call to mind* and dwell on various Psalms, such as: Psalm 16; 23; 27; 62; 63; 73:23-28; 84.

In addition, think about **Mary**, in contrast to her sister **Martha** (Lk 10:38-42). Also, consider, again, the many things listed in the section above, as these often hinder a personal relationship with God.

• *Lacking Joy & Peace*

When you are lacking contentment, peace, and joy, *call to mind* God and how much He has done for you—especially how much He has forgiven you, and how He loves you. Also, think about the woman who was overflowing with joy and gratitude because she was keenly aware of how much she was given, and forgiven, by Jesus (Lk 7:36-50).

In addition, *call to mind* several verses that exhort us to *give thanks* and *be grateful*—not necessarily *about* our circumstances—but to always give thanks *in* all our circumstances (Col 3:15-16; 4:2; 1 Thess 5:16-18; Ps 100; 105:1-5; cp. Rom 1:21). We also have a lengthy list elsewhere on over one hundred truths about who we are and what we have in Christ, which produces hope, comfort, joy, and peace.

And, as if all that is not enough, *call to mind* and ruminate on the truths and directives in Phil 4:4-13 and in passages such as: Neh 8:10; Ps 16; Prov 10:28; Rom 15:13; Gal 5:22-23; 1 Pet 1:8-9

Brief daily devotional: *31 Ways To Know True & Lasting Peace*

• *In Deep Sorrow*

When you are in the midst of deep sorrow, you can *call to mind* the insights and cries of the many **Psalmists** (Ps 18:1-6; 25:16-22; 27:1-4; 34:18; 56:3-4; 62; 63:3; Ps 73:23-26; 145:18; 147:3), as well as other verses (Matt 5:4; Jn 16:33; 2 Cor 4:16-18; 6:10; 1 Pet 5:6-7). [For more, see the last section on suffering and trauma.]

• *Dominated By Circumstances*

When you are overwhelmed by painful situations in life, you can *call to mind* these four words from 2 Corinthians 6:10: "*sorrowful, yet always rejoicing.*" This reminds us that we are not *stuck* in painful, or even horrible circumstances—and that, while we can and should be sorrowful in certain distressing situations, we can *always* rejoice as well (see also Phil 4:4-13; 1 Thess 5:16-18; Ps 37; 73:15ff).

Another possible change to work on here starts with this question: to what degree do you focus way too much on your circumstances (good or bad ones), while neglecting the blessings and realities that transcend your circumstances? The "easier said than done" solution here is to set your mind and heart less and less on what is temporary (i.e., your circumstances), and more and more on God, His love, His grace, His Word, His ways, and those things which are eternal (cp. Col 3:1-4; Phil 1:21; 4:4-13; Hab 3:17-19; Ps 37; 73:15-26; Matt 6:19-21; 2 Cor 4:16-18; Heb 10:32-12:13).

- *Faulty Thinking of "It's Never Enough" or "I'm not enough"*

When we have these erroneous ideas pass through our minds, then this is a likely sign of a very common struggle: we are living according to a *guilt-based* or *performance-based* mindset *as if* we are under the Old Covenant. Therefore, when you are troubled with these thoughts —by feelings of worthlessness, unworthiness, and hopelessness— and by the thought that "No matter how much I do, it is never enough," then *call to mind*, dwell on, and live in the *New Covenant*—especially the reality of *the sufficiency of God*, and *our sufficiency in Him* and His grace, truth, and love.

While all of that is beautiful and true, we also need to acknowledge this truth: *we* are not enough—that is, apart from God. However, in Him, and through His grace and mercy, we have all the love and value we will ever need, and more. Therefore, when we call to mind these supreme truths—and believe and delight in them—we can be secure, knowing we have all that we need (2 Cor 3:5ff; 9:8; Eph 3:16ff; Gal 3:1ff; Col 2:10; 2 Pet 1:3-4; 2 Tim 1:7; 3:15-17).

- *Intrusive Thoughts*

When you are struggling with unwanted and invasive thoughts of any kind, then *call to mind* Jeremiah's wonderful response: "Yet *this* I call to mind and *therefore I have hope*" (Lam 3:21ff).

In addition, when it comes to the bigger picture of being re-minded, changing your heart, and getting rid of any strongholds, you can call to mind 2 Corinthians 10:3-5, and work on the overall solution of taking "captive" unwanted thoughts and faulty thinking, and making them "obedient to Christ."

In other words, Jesus is the Word of truth (Jn 1:1)—and He is *the* way, *the* truth, and *the* life (Jn 14:6)—and so we can increasingly replace our erroneous or intrusive thoughts with the truth, particularly the truth of God's Word, as well as His love and grace. While we all have a need to do this, keep in mind, however, that it is very common for these unwanted thoughts to be connected to our need to forgive.

Therefore, when it comes to a matter where this is needed, make sure you handled these unwanted thoughts in the context of forgiveness (Eph 4:31-32). See also: Ps 1:1-3; 27:4; 94:19; Prov 4:20-27; Rom 8:5-6; 12:2; 13:14; 2 Cor 3:5-18; 5:17; 6:10; Eph 4:22-24; Phil 4:6-8; Col 3:1-4, 16-17; 2 Tim 1:7: Heb 12:1-2

- *Trauma*

When in the midst of intense suffering, or when past trauma rears its ugly head, then you can *call to mind* one or more key verses that you have personalized, and have already applied to your heart.

In addition, here are numerous verses you can look to, dwell on, identify with, learn, model, and rely on to help you *process your past pain with God*: Ps 2-7; 9-13; 16-18; 20; 22; 23; 25; 27-31; 33-35; 37-45; 51; 52; 54-57; 59-64; 68-74; 79; 80; 82-84; 86; 88; 90; 91; 94; 102; 103; 107; 108; 109; 110; 112; 116; 118; 120; 121; 123; 125; 130; 131; 132; 138; 139; 140-147; Lam 1-5.

We all experience suffering, pain, and trauma in varying degrees—some people more than others. However, we often experience worsening sadness, distress, hopelessness, and anxiety if we do not appropriately grieve and process traumatic events, or the loss we experience in our life. Not doing so generally results in what is often described as "PTSD" (Post-Traumatic Stress Disorder). However, while the pain and stress is all too real, this plight should not be labeled as a "disorder." Rather, it is an understandable, if not natural and expected, outcome when we experience trauma, *but* do not truly grieve and process our pain. Ironically, being labeled with a "disorder" frequently causes a great deal of distress, hurt, confusion, discouragement, and hopelessness.

Fortunately, there is good news: there are solutions. We do not have to be stuck here. While this severe suffering is best dealt with *proactively* (i.e., processing our grief, especially with God), we also need to be sufficiently prepared to handle this *reactively* (i.e., responding well when we are reminded of past suffering, which is often referred to as being "triggered").

Unfortunately, there is no quick fix here, particularly when it comes to the more painful things in our lives. Nevertheless, not only can we overcome these, we can and will grow in amazing ways as well (someone coined the term, "Post-Traumatic *Growth*," yet this reality has been around for thousands of years; e.g., the Psalms; Lamentations).

And, of course, there are times when it is wise to approach this with the help of others. In addition to all this, and as discussed a few times already, the biblical understanding and application of forgiveness is often much of the solution here.

APPLICATION & DISCUSSION

+ What are at least 5 things that stand out to you the most from the previous list?

+ What are the specific areas you need to work on proactively and reactively?

Above and through all this, it is critical to remember that we cannot just *reactively* call these truths to mind and expect that our problems will be resolved. While this might help in a pinch, a reactionary approach can easily turn into behaviorism, and into a dependency on coping techniques.

What is more, not only can this cheapen God's Word (if we use Scripture to merely distract ourselves, or to just cope), we are failing to address *the cause* of our struggles. As a result, this will not produce true growth, nor will it lead to an actual heart change (cp. Matt 15:7-9).

Therefore, we need to do the heavy lifting *in advance*, not just in the heat of the moment. This means that we need to *proactively* think through and increasingly understand, *believe*, and apply these truths to our hearts. As we *prepare our minds*, these life-producing principles will be increasingly effective in helping us transform our hearts and renew our minds.

> *Do not conform to the pattern of this world,*
> *but* **be transformed by the renewing of your mind.**
>
> — ROMANS 12:2

+ The first thing to do is to identify the specific areas you struggle in the most. Which of these have you identified in your life (e.g., anxiety; guilt; being troubled in mind; temptation; suffering)?

Next, make sure you spend a generous amount of time *beforehand* diving into, studying, meditating on, delighting in, *truly believing* and resting in the biblical truths associated with these things.

+ Which Scriptures pique your interest the most? Why those verses?

Finally, to go even deeper, you can look up these passages in their context. In addition, you can cross-reference other similar verses (i.e., looking up the various verses throughout Scripture on the same subject like peace of mind; love; suffering). This will greatly enhance your understanding, as well as your general peace, comfort, and security.

Over all of this, you need to prayerfully ruminate on and seek to grow in *your belief* of these truths, and God Himself. And then—as you believe and store up these truths in your heart—they will be exceedingly helpful at those pivotal moments.

> *The good man brings good things out of the good stored up in his heart ...*
>
> — LUKE 6:45 [NIV]

15

PROACTIVE & REACTIVE
HELPFUL RE-MINDERS

All Scripture is given by inspiration of God, and is profitable for doctrine, for reproof, for correction, for instruction in righteousness, *that the man of God may be complete,* **thoroughly equipped for every good work.**

— 2 TIMOTHY 3:16-17

Another powerful tool for your growth and for being re-minded is to write down, perhaps on 3x5 cards, the Scriptures you highly value—which also speak to your specific struggles—and will generally strengthen and bless you. In addition, try to keep them easily accessible.

As we have already discussed, two things are necessary here—being both proactive and reactive.

Proactive: You need to think about, learn from, and enjoy these Scriptures *proactively*. This means spending ample time reading, studying, applying, meditating on, and believing these verses—and deepening your faith in and relationship with God.

Reactive: You need to rely on these verses *reactively*. This means *calling them to mind* when you are stressed, anxious, depressed, feeling condemned, etc.

As you proactively grow in your understanding of these truths—and as you deepen your belief in them (i.e., proactively)—you will become more and more equipped (2 Tim 3:16-17). Then, as a result, these verses will be exceedingly helpful to you when you are under stress, as you call these truths to mind reactively.

In addition, the more you do the proactive *and* reactive work, the more your heart will be strengthened, the more comfort and freedom you will enjoy, and the more you will become like Jesus (Eph 4:22-5:2; Gal 4:19; Rom 12:2).

Here, again, is our highlighted example of someone *responding well* to anxiety, hopelessness, and pain from the past.

*Yet **this** I call to mind and therefore I have hope ...*

— LAMENTATIONS 3:21 [NIV]

What Jeremiah called to mind just so happens to be some of the most beautiful truths about God, His grace, His faithfulness, and His love for us. When it comes to life-giving verses, "this" would make a great addition to your collection of Scripture:

Because of the Lord's great love
we are not consumed,
for His compassions never fail.
They are new every morning;

> *great is Your faithfulness.*
> *I say to myself, "The Lord is my portion;*
> *therefore I will wait for Him."*
> *The Lord is good to those whose hope is in Him,*
> *to the one who seeks Him.*
>
> — LAMENTATIONS 3:22-25 [NIV]

+ What are some other pertinent verses that you would like to have stored up in your heart, and have handy on 3x5 cards?

What is *the* greatest and most important truth for believers? What might help us be *re-minded* in the best possible way? While there are many good answers to choose from, I believe the right one is this: **the sufficiency of God and His Word** (e.g., 2 Pet 1:3-4; 2 Tim 3:15-17; Ps 19:7-11).

Put another way, knowing, believing, resting in, and living in this reality will bring about more peace, security, and joy than any other truth. Why? Because, when it comes to knowing a sufficient amount of love, strength, blessings, comfort, and security, we have all that we need in God alone—particularly through His love, grace, power, and Word of truth. And remember that the belief and fruit here will take *time* to grow.

With that in mind, the following verses are suggestions for you to grow in knowing God's character—especially His sufficiency—and His glorious and all-sufficient love for you. Therefore, make sure you dedicate ample time to meditate on and delight in these incredible truths about God and His love for us—and how He Himself, often through His Word of life, gives us everything we need for life, godliness, peace, and salvation.

> *His divine power has given us **everything we need for life and godliness** through our knowledge of him who called us by his own glory and goodness. Through these he has given us his very great and precious*

promises, *so that through them you may participate in the divine nature and escape the corruption in the world caused by evil desires.*

— 2 PETER 1:3-4 [NIV]

The beloved of the Lord shall dwell in safety by Him, Who shelters him all the day long; and he shall dwell between His shoulders.

— DEUTERONOMY 33:12

But you are a forgiving God, gracious and compassionate, slow to anger and abounding in love.

— NEHEMIAH 9:17 [NIV]

Blessed is the man who walks *not* in the counsel of the ungodly, nor stands in the path of sinners, nor sits in the seat of the scornful; but **his delight is in the law of the Lord, and in His law he meditates day and night.** He shall be like a tree planted by the rivers of water, that brings forth its fruit in its season, whose leaf also shall not wither; and **whatever he does shall prosper.**

— PSALM 1:1-3

As for God, **His way is perfect**; the word of the Lord is proven; He is a shield to all who trust in Him.

— PSALM 18:30

The law of the Lord is **perfect**, *reviving the soul*. The statutes of the Lord are trustworthy, making wise the simple. The precepts of the Lord are right, *giving joy to the heart*. The commands of the Lord are radiant, giving light to the eyes. The fear of the Lord is pure, enduring forever.

Re-Minded

The ordinances of the Lord are sure and altogether righteous. They are more precious than gold, than much pure gold; they are sweeter than honey, than honey from the comb. By them is your servant warned; in keeping them there is great reward.

— PSALM 19:7-11

You prepare a table before me in the presence of my enemies; You anoint my head with oil; my cup runs over. Surely goodness and mercy shall follow me all the days of my life; and I will dwell in the house of the Lord forever.

— PSALM 23:5-6

One thing I have desired of the Lord, that will I seek: that I may dwell in the house of the Lord all the days of my life, to behold the beauty of the Lord, and to inquire in His temple.

— PSALM 27:4

For the word of the Lord is right, and all His work is done in truth. He loves righteousness and justice; the earth is full of the goodness of the Lord.

— PSALM 33:4-5

Behold, the eye of the Lord is on those who fear Him, on those who hope in His mercy, to deliver their soul from death, and to keep them alive in famine. Our soul waits for the Lord; He is our help and our shield. For our heart shall rejoice in Him, because we have trusted in His holy name. Let Your mercy, O Lord, be upon us, just as we hope in You.

— PSALM 33:18-22

The Lord is my Shepherd; I shall not want.

— PSALM 23:1

Oh, taste and see that the Lord is good; blessed is the man who trusts in Him! Oh, fear the Lord, you His saints! There is no want to those who fear Him. The young lions lack and suffer hunger; but those who seek the Lord shall not lack any good thing.

— PSALM 34:8-10

Your mercy, O Lord, is in the heavens; Your faithfulness reaches to the clouds. Your righteousness is like the great mountains; Your judgments are a great deep; O Lord, You preserve man and beast. How precious is Your lovingkindness, O God! Therefore the children of men put their trust under the shadow of Your wings. They are abundantly satisfied with the fullness of Your house, and You give them drink from the river of Your pleasures. For with You is the fountain of life; in Your light we see light.

— PSALM 36:5-9

Trust in the Lord, and do good; dwell in the land, and feed on His faithfulness. *Delight yourself also in the Lord*, and He shall give you the desires of your heart.

— PSALM 37:3-4

Blessed is that man who makes the Lord his trust, and does not respect the proud, nor such as turn aside to lies. Many, O Lord my God, are Your wonderful works which You have done; and Your thoughts toward us cannot be recounted to You in order; if I would declare and speak of them, they are more than can be numbered.

— PSALM 40:4-5

Re-Minded

My soul, wait silently for *God alone*, for my expectation is from Him. He only is my rock and my salvation; He is my defense; I shall not be moved. In God is my salvation and my glory; the rock of my strength, and my refuge, is in God. Trust in Him at all times, you people; pour out your heart before Him; God is a refuge for us. Selah

— PSALM 62:5-8

So I have looked for You in the sanctuary, to see Your power and Your glory. Because *Your lovingkindness is better than life*, my lips shall praise You. Thus I will bless You while I live; I will lift up my hands in Your name. My soul shall be satisfied as with marrow and fatness, and my mouth shall praise You with joyful lips.

— PSALM 63:2-5

For a day in Your courts is better than a thousand. I would rather be a doorkeeper in the house of my God than dwell in the tents of wickedness. For the Lord God is a sun and shield; the Lord will give grace and glory; no good thing will He withhold from those who walk uprightly.

— PSALM 84:10-11

Oh, that men would give thanks to the Lord for His goodness, and for His wonderful works to the children of men! For He satisfies the longing soul, and fills the hungry soul with goodness.

— PSALM 107:8-9

I wait for the Lord, my soul waits, and *in His word I do hope*.

My soul waits for the Lord more than those who watch for the morning—yes, more than those who watch for the morning.

O Israel, hope in the Lord; for with the Lord there is mercy, and with Him is abundant redemption.

— PSALM 130:5-7

You will keep him in *perfect peace*, whose mind is stayed on You, because he trusts in You.

— ISAIAH 26:3

But those who wait on the Lord shall renew their strength; they shall mount up with wings like eagles, they shall run and not be weary, they shall walk and not faint.

— ISAIAH 40:31

Ho! Everyone who thirsts, come to the waters; and you who have no money, come, buy and eat. Yes, come, buy wine and milk without money and without price. *Why do you spend money for what is not bread, and your wages for what does not satisfy?* Listen carefully to Me, and eat what is good, *and let your soul delight itself in abundance.* Incline your ear, and come to Me. Hear, and your soul shall live.

— ISAIAH 55:1-3

For My thoughts are not your thoughts, nor are your ways My ways," says the Lord. For as the heavens are higher than the earth, so are My ways higher than your ways, and My thoughts than your thoughts.

— ISAIAH 55:8-9

For with God nothing will be impossible.

— LUKE 1:37

Blessed is the man who trusts in the Lord, and whose hope is the Lord. For he shall be like a tree planted by the waters, which spreads out its roots by the river, and will not fear when heat comes; but its leaf will be green, and will not be anxious in the year of drought, nor will cease from yielding fruit.

— JEREMIAH 17:7-8

Ah, Lord God! Behold, You have made the heavens and the earth by Your great power and outstretched arm. *There is nothing too hard for You.*

— JEREMIAH 32:17

The Lord your God in your midst, the Mighty One, will save; He will rejoice over you with gladness, He will quiet you with His love, He will rejoice over you with singing.

— ZEPHANIAH 3:17

Jesus answered and said to her, "Whoever drinks of this water will thirst again, but whoever drinks of the water that I shall give him will never thirst. But the water that I shall give him will become in him *a fountain of water springing up into everlasting life.*

— JOHN 4:13 -14

On the last day, that great day of the feast, Jesus stood and cried out, saying, "If anyone thirsts, let him come to Me and drink. He who believes in Me, as the Scripture has said, out of his heart will flow rivers of living water."

— JOHN 7:38

If you abide in Me, and *My words abide in you*, you will ask what you desire, and it shall be done for you. By this My Father is glorified, that you bear much fruit; so you will be My disciples.

— JOHN 15:7-8

Now hope does not disappoint, because *the love of God has been poured out in our hearts* by the Holy Spirit who was given to us.

— ROMANS 5:5

For if by the one man's offense death reigned through the one, much more those who receive abundance of grace and of the gift of righteousness will reign in life through the One, Jesus Christ.

— ROMANS 5:17

Moreover the law entered that the offense might abound. *But where sin abounded, grace abounded much more.*

— ROMANS 5:20

What then shall we say to these things? If God is for us, who can be against us? He who did not spare His own Son, but delivered Him up for us all, *how shall He not with Him also freely give us all things*?

— ROMANS 8:31-32

Yet in all these things *we are more than conquerors through Him who loved us*. For I am persuaded that neither death nor life, nor angels nor principalities nor powers, nor things present nor things to come, nor height nor depth, nor any other created thing, shall be able to separate us from the love of God which is in Christ Jesus our Lord.

— ROMANS 8:37-39

For Christ is the end of the law for righteousness to everyone who believes.

— ROMANS 10:4

For whatever things were written before were written for our learning, that we *through the patience and comfort of the Scriptures might have hope.*

— ROMANS 15:4

Now may the God of hope fill you with all joy and peace in believing, *that you may abound in hope* by the power of the Holy Spirit.

— ROMANS 15:13

I thank my God always concerning you for the grace of God which was given to you by Christ Jesus, that you were enriched in everything by Him in all utterance and all knowledge, even as the testimony of Christ was confirmed in you, so that you come short in no gift, eagerly waiting for the revelation of our Lord Jesus Christ,

— 1 CORINTHIANS 1:4-7

Now we have received, not the spirit of the world, but the Spirit who is from God, *that we might know the things that have been freely given to us by God.*

— 1 CORINTHIANS 2:12

And God is able to make *all grace abound toward you,* that you, *always having all sufficiency in all things,* may have an abundance for every good work.

— 2 CORINTHIANS 9:8

And He said to me, *"My grace is sufficient for you,* for My strength is made perfect in weakness." Therefore most gladly I will rather boast in my infirmities, that the power of Christ may rest upon me.

— 2 CORINTHIANS 12:9

Blessed be the God and Father of our Lord Jesus Christ, *who has blessed us with every spiritual blessing in the heavenly places in Christ…*

— EPHESIANS 1:3

…that He would grant you, according to the riches of His glory, to be strengthened with might through His Spirit in the inner man, that Christ may dwell in your hearts through faith; that you, being rooted and grounded in love, may be able to comprehend with all the saints what is the width and length and depth and height—*to know the love of Christ which passes knowledge; that you may be filled with all the fullness of God.*

Now to Him who is able to do *exceedingly abundantly above all that we ask or think*, according to the power that works in us, to Him be glory in the church by Christ Jesus to all generations, forever and ever. Amen.

— EPHESIANS 3:16-21

Not that I speak in regard to need, for I have learned in whatever state I am, to be content: I know how to be abased, and I know how to abound. Everywhere and in all things I have learned both to be full and to be hungry, both to abound and to suffer need. I can do all things through Christ who strengthens me.

— PHILIPPIANS 4:11-13

And *my God shall supply all your need according to His riches in glory* by Christ Jesus.

— PHILIPPIANS 4:19

For in Him dwells all the fullness of the Godhead bodily; and *you are complete in Him*, who is the head of all principality and power.

— COLOSSIANS 2:9-10

Command those who are rich in this present age not to be haughty, nor to trust in uncertain riches but in the living God, *who gives us richly all things to enjoy.*

— 1 TIMOTHY 6:17

All Scripture is given by inspiration of God, and is profitable for doctrine, for reproof, for correction, for instruction in righteousness, *that the man of God may be complete, thoroughly equipped for every good work.*

— 2 TIMOTHY 3:16-17

16

FINAL FOCUS

Finally, brethren, whatever things are *true*, whatever things are *noble*, whatever things are *just*, whatever things are *pure*, whatever things are *lovely*, whatever things are *of good report*, if there is any *virtue* and if there is *anything praiseworthy—**meditate on these things**.* The things which you learned and received and heard and saw in me, these do, **and the God of peace will be with you.**

— PHILIPPIANS 4:8-9

In God's Word, we have learned numerous life-changing truths highlighted throughout this book. In fact, not only is there an abundance of vital principles here, there are hundreds of verses to continually draw from and apply to our hearts and lives.

More specifically, we have focused on and learned what it is to be *reminded*. We have also learned how to put this into practice so that we can continually grow, change our hearts, and overcome many of life's challenges.

Re-Minded = Renewing our minds by calling to mind and believing in our hearts the many biblical truths about God, love, grace, forgiveness, etc.

Along with that, here are ten more key principles or themes to remember and apply to your life.

10 Focus Principles

1. Call To Mind

A great deal of our troubles and the unwanted fruit in our lives would be lessened or removed—*and* replaced with incredible fruit —if everyone somehow fully lived by the principles in *just one verse*: Lamentations 3:21, which allows us to rely on God and all the other truths and verses in Scripture.

2. Live It Out

In addition, if the biblical principles in this one verse were somehow truly lived by everyone, then the need for counseling would be greatly reduced (which shows the power of God and His Word in our lives, and the abundance of help and blessings He gives us in Himself, and in Scripture).

3. Press On

Our present experience is not determined by our past experience.

4. Choose Wisely

Most of the fruit in our life is *not* determined by what happens to us —but by *how we choose to respond*, by *what we choose to set our mind on*, by *what we believe*, by *where we choose to put our hope*, and by *our overall relationship with God*.

5. Be Re-Minded

Everyone needs to be re-minded, both proactively and in times of trouble.

6. Process Biblically

God gives us numerous ways we can truly grieve and process the pain, loss, and trauma in our lives, and we all need to walk this path more than once.

7. Check Your Fruit

The fruit in our life is *an invaluable window to our soul*.

8. Understand The Purpose of Feelings

God designed us to experience unwanted and painful feelings—and He did so out of love for us, and to protect us, direct us, and bless us.

9. Respond Well

Much of our life and wellbeing depends on how well we understand and respond to this divine design.

10. Structure Your Day

Structuring our day—particularly the first and last hour or so of the day—is essential to being *re-minded*, strengthened, blessed, and in overcoming countless troubles in life.

With all this (and much more) available to you, please continue to persevere in consistently being *re-minded*, and in doing the hard work of heart work. While this can be very challenging, you will be so glad as you faithfully apply these truths to your heart and mind.

Not only will you grow and be strengthened, but you will produce more and more of the desired fruit in your life—as you bless God and others in a multitude of ways.

HOPE FOR LIFE | RESOURCES

- Love + Discernment: Why We Need Both
- Forgiveness: A Biblical Handbook
- Forgiveness & Trust
- Overcoming Anxiety: How To Replace Fear With Peace
- Counterfeits: The Enemy's Greatest Weapon
- Biblical Discernment
- Why The Truth Matters
- Enablers: Enabling Dysfunction Or Enabling Reconciliation
- Trustworthy People: How To Spot One + How To Be One
- Thinking Biblically About Narcissism
- Our Greatest Danger

Find these books and more at HopeForLifeOnline.com

ABOUT THE AUTHOR

Mark Baker has been a full-time biblical counselor for over two decades, and is passionate about equipping people with the life-giving hope found in God's perfect, all-sufficient Word. He is a prolific author and teacher on a wide range of subjects, including relationships, conflict, forgiveness, marriage, counseling, and discernment.

Mark lives in California's Central Valley with his wife, Emily and their family, where he is the director of Hope For Life Biblical Counseling & Equipping, a non-profit ministry serving the local community and the worldwide church at large.

For more books and resources:
HopeForLifeOnline.com

NOTES

4. The Hard Work of Heart Work

1. Spurgeon, Charles Haddon, *Morning & Evening*, (1866-1868)
2. Elliot, Elisabeth, *Passion & Purity*, (1984: Baker Publishing)

7. Right Focus

1. BacktotheBible.org, quoting source: https://www.cbelabs.org/power-of-4

8. Distracted Focus

1. Muller, George, *The Autobiography of George Muller*, (1805–1898)
2. Muller, George, *The Autobiography of George Muller*, (1805–1898)
3. Elliot, Elisabeth, *Gateway To Joy Radio Broadcast*, (1988-2001)

11. Caution About Counterfeits

1. Carl McColman, *The Big Book of Christian Mysticism: The Essential Guide to Contemplative Spirituality*, (2010, Hampton Roads Publishing; pp. 63-64, emphasis added)
2. Jager, Willigis, *Contemplation*, (1994: Liguori; cited in *A Time of Departing*; Yungen; p. 31, emphasis added)
3. McLaren, Brian, cited in: *The Berean Call* (Feb. 1, 2008) *Evangelical Mysticism?*, T.A. McMahon, https://www.thebereancall.org/content/evangelical-mysticism
4. Keating, Thomas, *Finding Grace At The Center*, (1978) cited by Lighthouse Trails: https://www.lighthousetrailsresearch.com/blog/lectio-divina-what-it-is-what-it-is-not-and-should-christians-practice-it-2/
5. Yungen, Ray, *A Time of Departing: How Ancient Mystical Practices Are Uniting Christians With The World's Religions* (2020: Lighthouse Trails Publishing)

13. Night & Day

1. Ryle, John Charles (1816-1900), Bishop of Liverpool, cited at: https://www.azquotes.com/author/17287-J_C_Ryle
2. Muller, George, *The Autobiography of George Muller*, (1805–1898)

Printed in Great Britain
by Amazon